TEACHING ABOUT SOCIAL ISSUES
IN AMERICAN HISTORY

Four Demonstration Lessons

by

Allan O. Kownslar

Social Science Education Consortium, Inc.

ERIC Clearinghouse for Social Studies/Social Science Education

Boulder, Colorado

1978

ORDERING INFORMATION

This publication is available from:

Social Science Education Consortium, Inc.
855 Broadway
Boulder, Colorado 80302

ISBN 0-89994-230-X

Price: $8.95

This publication was prepared with funding from the National
Institute of Education, U.S. Department of Health, Education,
and Welfare under contract no. 400-78-0006. The opinions
expressed in this report do not necessarily reflect the
positions or policies of NIE or HEW.

TABLE OF CONTENTS

PREFACE

As every journalist knows, most people are fascinated by controversy. The fact that every new development in a "Karen Anne Quinlan case" or an "Allan Bakke case" rates a headline article and prominent mention in the evening newscast is sometimes lamented by observers who fear that media overkill is distorting our sense of perspective. Yet there is no doubt that intensive press coverage breeds, at least, familiarity--in 1978, for example, there probably were few literate Americans who could not identify Allan Bakke and describe his grievance against the U.C. Davis Medical School.

This kind of public awareness can be a boon to teachers, especially teachers of American history. Students who yawn at the very thought of the Hawley-Smoot Tariff Act will jump eagerly into a discussion of the proposed Equal Rights Amendment--an issue that seems, with some justification, to have more relevance to their lives. Furthermore, as the author of this volume points out, the pedagogical arguments for teaching about contemporary issues in social studies courses are most persuasive. Thus the question, for many teachers, is not "Should we do it?" but "How can we do it most effectively?"

Allan O. Kownslar, a gifted and prolific history curriculum writer, has published a variety of resources for teaching about modern controversies. The four sample lessons in this volume were prepared in the spring of 1978 by 16 students in Kownslar's history teaching methods class at Trinity University in San Antonio, Texas. After being tested in the Alamo Heights Independent School District and at Texas Military Institute, the lessons were revised, brought up to date, and integrated with rationale statements and additional background material. We hope that the resulting volume will prove to be a valuable resource for incorporating the teaching of social issues into an American history course.

James E. Davis
Associate Director, Social Science Education
Consortium, Inc., and ERIC Clearinghouse for
Social Studies/Social Science Education

The author wishes to thank Curtis Cox, John Cunningham, Joanne Furtek, and Frieda Krueger for their cooperation in field testing many of the activities contained in these lessons. In addition, a very special thanks is due to Marguerite L. Kownslar and Ann M. Williams for their editorial comments and guidance.

I. INTRODUCTION

WHY TEACH ABOUT SOCIAL ISSUES?

has been a dominant characteristic of American education
of the Massachusetts Old Deluder Law in 1647. Most new
ideas, however, have attracted a fair amount of controversy.
past 20 years, this has been particularly true in the area of
udies instruction. One innovation that has created a great deal
has been the introduction of modern-day issues into secondary-
rican history courses.

the 1950s one could search in vain among the best-selling his-
or in-depth material about the embryo civil rights movement.
blacks were mentioned in texts, they were few in number.
bers of other minority groups received the same kind of cur-
nt. Generally, what students were handed was an Anglo/male-
dominated American history presented so blandly that one could easily
come to the conclusion that our national past was entirely benign and
happy. Slavery, the Civil War, Reconstruction, American expansionism,
the Great Depression, labor strife, minority problems, Korea—these and
other contentious topics, apparently, were not considered part of the
"real story."

The ensuing decade brought some changes, in textbook approaches as
well as in pedagogy, that reflected a growing dissatisfaction with the
lack of debatable issues in the study of U.S. history. Some textbook
programs and an increasing number of teachers began to include more than
just the "good" side of our past. Not only problems and dilemmas associated with early events but also those of the modern era began to be
seen as a vital part of American history. Curriculum materials became
available which focused on the civil rights movement of the 1960s, the
contributions and problems of cultural minorities, the influential roles
played by American women, U.S. involvement in conflicts all over the globe,
ethics in government, and the extension of basic guarantees established
by the Constitution, by laws, and by court rulings. More and more, presentations of controversial topics included the points of view of both
proponents and opponents.[1]

The introduction of controversial and contemporary topics into U.S.

history classes and the reemphasis on inquiry and values clarification as approaches to studying the American past provoked substantial criticism. Some critics publicly protested against certain programs; others made their views known through articles in scholarly journals. Many of these critics charged that the so-called newer trends in social studies education placed too much emphasis on conflict as a societal change agent. Though they admitted that conflict has certainly existed in this country and that at times it may have had an immediate effect on public policy, they insisted that conflict was not the basis of our democratic society. "The vitality of our society has been and continues to be compromise, not conflict," one critic argued. Through compromise, he went on, "the desires of the many can be reconciled to accommodate the needs and rights of all. Although compromise may be slow, it is both healthy and sure. These are qualities that conflict change does not have."[2]

In response to such criticism, some historians pointed out that any accurate study of American history must contain materials and teaching strategies designed to help students discover that conflict has been an important factor in shaping our democracy. For example, to whom might we now swear allegiance if there had been no American Revolution of 1776? Who might now rule the Texans if they had not rebelled against Santa Anna's dictatorial powers in 1836? In both these situations, conflict secured results that were both immediate and lasting; from such conflicts came much of the foundation on which our political structure rests today. Though compromise was one result of those conflicts, even in compromising we did not sacrifice our basic political values; we compromised only on the ways and means to implement those values into governmental policy that would serve the best interests of society.[3]

One could also add that throughout our history there have been certain individuals--among them Thomas Jefferson, Paul Revere, Abraham Lincoln, Jefferson Davis, Robert E. Lee, Susan B. Anthony, Martin Luther King, Jr., and Cesar Chavez--who have refused to compromise their basic and cherished ideals. When values are compromised, democracy has sometimes suffered--as witness the results of the Yalta agreement or of our decision to allow the creation of a divided Berlin. Students who are capable of comprehending the abstractions and concepts involved in such examples should be able to look at any given issue and consider whether conflict, compromise, or both may be required.[4]

Critics of the values-clarification-oriented social studies materials developed during the past two decades have maintained that the emphasis of those materials on the supremacy of individual rights is unreasonable. One such critic, James M. Benjamin, argued that the essence of a democratic society is that it "strives to maintain a delicate balance between the rights of the individual and the reasonable interests of the society." Indeed, he continued, consistent emphasis can be placed on one of these interests only at the expense of the other: "Unless the young secure a sure understanding of the need for that balance, our society will lack the necessary order to avoid continuous conflict. Without order we will find it increasingly difficult to make decisions, either in our personal lives or at the ballot box, that will enhance life for all."[5]

Other educators believe that values clarification can play a vital role in the study of issues involving such conflicts as the everpresent dilemma of whether individual rights should take precedence over group rights. To provide undue emphasis on either individual or group rights in the classroom would not only be unreasonable, it would be alien to our political traditions.[6]

Defenders of its use in the classroom claim that values clarification does not mean the imposition of a value system but is, instead, an attempt to encourage students to carefully reexamine, explain, and justify whatever values they cherish. If the issue at hand involves a clash of interests between the rights of an individual and those of society in general, appropriate values-clarification activities would require students to articulate the possible short-term and long-term results of the positions they choose to take.[7]

Another point of contention about recent trends in the teaching of history has been focused on what some educators regard as an undue emphasis on the "humanizing" of historical figures. Although stressing that historical figures had "feet of clay" may make them seem more human, James Benjamin pointed out, one of the purposes of examining the lives of famous people is to recognize that people can rise above their mere "humanness." These critics feel that more attention ought to be paid to the "good" accomplished by people who have helped ensure the continuation of human civilization. The fact that many of our famous figures "sometimes faltered in their personal lives, while titillating, is hardly adequate history nor even worthwhile knowledge for the young," Benjamin observed.

Even supporters of the "humanizing" strategy admit that it is best reserved for mature secondary-level students, and that teachers should also emphasize that throughout history some remarkable individuals have transcended their "humanness." Indeed, to study the lives of such people as George Washington, John Adams, Sam Houston, Chester A. Arthur, Eleanor Roosevelt, Audie Murphy, and Harry Truman is to realize that, in spite of their frailties and temptations, many human beings are capable of accomplishing much more than is expected of them. If students are not shown the shortcomings as well as the strengths of historical figures, as adults they may become cynical and disillusioned when they discover that many of their contemporary "idols" also have "feet of clay." Sensible teachers, many educators have observed, have always tended to present historical figures without overemphasizing either their strengths or their weaknesses.[9]

Along the same lines, some critics have argued that education currently tends to overemphasize the inadequacies of American society, past and present. "Our history is full of error, and inhumanness cannot be disputed," said one such critic, "but it ought to be carefully balanced with the knowledge that our society has always been self-examining and has worked for correction. After all, a democratic society is a becoming society, not a perfect one. Only dictatorships claim perfection."[10]

Yet who can deny that the story of our nation has been one in which men and women have labored long and diligently to overcome inadequacies? Our federal and state constitutions, the Bill of Rights, the abolition of slavery, restrictions on monopoly power, suffrage for blacks, women, and tenants, laws protecting children, guarantees of civil rights for all groups--all these benefits are the result of efforts to solve existing problems. The fact that Americans have overcome such problems should serve as an inspiration to future generations as they cope with new dilemmas and new problems.[11]

During the 1960s a different kind of criticism of the teaching of

American history came from many of the young leftists. They charged that teachers' failure to include a variety of contemporary topics in the social studies curriculum made study of the past irrelevant. This attitude, coupled with the career orientation of many students in the 1970s, helped cause a general decline of student interest in the study of our national past.

That such a decline exists was partly documented in 1975 by the Ad Hoc Committee on the Status of History in the Schools formed by members of the Organization of American Historians. After examining the situation extensively, these historians confirmed what many educators had suspected for years: The teaching of history was in trouble.

Parts of the committee's report show that in many school districts history is seen as being of secondary importance in comparison with other social sciences or humanities courses. Other sections describe how textbook orientation, with its "straight chronological . . . emphasis on dates" and "unimaginative presentation eschewing meaningful innovation and rational experimentation," has had a "stultifying effect on both the teacher and student . . . ." All in all, the report presents an array of data documenting the theory that enrollment in history classes declines at both secondary and college levels when satisfactory completion of certain history courses is no longer required for graduation, admission to a college, or teacher certification.[12]

Certain sections of the report seem to associate at least part of the decline in history classroom enrollments with the "new methodology." Although the term is never defined precisely in the report, the reader is given the impression that this new pedagogy concerns itself primarily with concept development and that it emphasizes recent history at the expense of a thorough examination of the past. Yet, if textbook sales are any indication of recent educational trends in social studies, probably not more than 15 percent of our schools have adopted such innovative programs. One could also argue that the use of many of these innovative programs has not hurt history as a discipline but, on the contrary, has made it more appealing and worthwhile to students.

Adding to the overall problems related to the teaching of American history is a movement that has recently received much attention in the

news media: the call for a return to the so-called basics. Some people
have proposed that social studies and history instruction return to the
time of 1957 and before, with emphasis placed only or mainly on recall,
however temporary, of certain data and on reading and writing skill development. This view was expressed by one member of a state board of
education when he stated, "I don't want any idea in [textbooks] that's
questionable."

Anyone looking at the back-to-basics movement would soon discover
that few social studies/history educators question the critical importance
of acquisition of data and development of reading and writing skills; such
knowledge and skills have always been essential ingredients for success
in and out of school. Yet people who would stress skill development while
ignoring the social studies innovations that have received so much emphasis during these past 20 years might keep in mind several things:

First, 1957, the year of Sputnik, was soon followed by far-reaching
scientific and technological changes that have continued to influence
our way of life. Whether we like it or not, these developments have
affected every aspect of the way we live, and education has been no exception.

Second, since the latter part of the 1950s many school districts have
also experienced changes, largely caused by shifting population patterns.
Changes in school populations create new educational needs that must be
met in a variety of new ways. For example, many teachers are discovering
that the traditional practice of using a single textbook for all the students at a given grade level is no longer workable.

Third, according to some specialists in educational trends, we now
have reason to believe that most students who enter the first grade in
September 1978 probably will, on reaching the twelfth grade, have been
exposed to at least four times as much knowledge as were those who began
school in September of 1966.

Obviously, then, public education in the 1970s is not the same as
it was in the 1950s. But why should it be? The field of medicine is
not the same, nor are the various fields of science. Who would seriously
consider going to a physician whose knowledge of medicine omitted any
development that happened later than 1957? It makes no more sense to ask

history teachers to ignore all the new studies and historical interpreta-
tions that have been added to the knowledge base during the last 20 years.

Finally, no matter how much all of us at times would like to return
to the supposedly simpler life of bygone days, no industrialized society
has ever been able to do so. Perhaps, too, Will Rogers was right when
he observed, "Things ain't what they used to be and probably never was."[14]

Many advocates of a back-to-basics approach have argued that education now puts far too much emphasis on the current and immediate, and
that if too many teachers "consistently consider the present without a
sure grasp of its historical roots, we are more likely to make mistakes
in ascertaining the value of a proposed action."[15] One reason for teaching social studies, say these observers, is to analyze historical experience in order to avoid making the same mistakes over and over again.

The OAH report to some degree echoed these sentiments, adding that
the present situation "seems to demand that historians be innovative in
order to be attractive." Although it was unlikely that historians could
ever "destroy the influence of presentism . . . ," the report observed,
its antihistorical consequences could be reduced "by demonstrating the
value of historical comparisons and the importance of a sense of time
and place."[16]

Many students probably would challenge the OAH committee's conclusion that there is too much presentism in history courses. Few history
survey courses, students might say, examine or even mention developments
after 1937. It is shocking to realize that at this writing 1937 was 41
years ago--a period greater than that comprising the presidential admin-
istrations of George Washington, John Adams, Thomas Jefferson, James
Madison, James Monroe, and John Quincy Adams. Forty-one years is also
more than a decade longer than the time from the French Revolution to
the defeat of Napoleon at Waterloo. Surely, students might argue, enough
time has elapsed so that teachers and students could begin to examine in
some depth the key events related to the World War II era.[17]

Supporters of presentism might also counter by pointing out that it
is not only possible but essential for any study of history to emphasize
current events and issues in the context of their relationships to the
past. Teachers can use an approach that moves from present-day problems

to parallel issues in the past and finally back to relevant current issues. The gap between two supposedly unrelated issues can thus be bridged by relating a contemporary problem to one in the past. Furthermore, moving from emotional (current) to contextual (past) to emotional (current) issues, students can more easily consider alternative value positions, since people often do not possess rigid ideas or attitudes about issues in the past. This method of examining historical issues can thus provide numerous opportunities for students to analyze value alternatives objectively before comparing them critically with their own values.

Proponents of the use of presentism say that this approach also provides a vehicle for teaching history "backward," whereby a class can begin with a contemporary issue of special concern, trace the historical causes of the problem or examine similar situations in the past, and finally compare past situations to today's problems. In so doing, students generally come to realize that neither problems nor proposed solutions are unique to the present.

It is obviously futile to attempt to educate students to be aggressive, independent inquirers if we force them to direct their curiosity exclusively toward the past. Whatever the area--be it grammar, auto mechanics, music, or history--unless the focus of inquiry seems in some way relevant to students (and to teachers), it is unlikely that any real learning will occur.[18]

The remainder of this monograph is devoted to methods for dealing with contemporary social and political issues in U.S. history classes at the secondary level. Many of these issues have not yet been incorporated into commercial textbook programs because, by their very nature, they stir up controversy--something most textbook publishers would prefer to avoid. As most Americans witnessed during the years 1954 to 1978, the dominant social-political issues of that time--as have such issues throughout our history--created considerable friction between and within large segments of our population. The turmoil created by those issues was evident in the discussions heard in places ranging from the neighborhood barbershop to the halls of Congress. Wherever such discussions occurred, whether they concerned civil rights, McCarthyism, U.S. involvement in Southeast Asia, law and order, patriotism, morality in government, or the back-to-basics educational movement, there obviously existed at least two sides to every issue.

Given the pervasiveness of the mass media, keeping social-political issues a secret from the youth of our nation clearly would be impossible. Young people watch television, and they cannot help but absorb at least some of what is said and pictured on the tube. Even if a student were isolated from radio, television, and newspapers, he or she could learn about a contemporary issue simply by listening to the conversations of peers, parents, or teachers.

The fact is that social-political issues are, consciously or sub-consciously, part of the knowledge students acquire, and this knowledge is reflected in the comments they make at home or at school. What is said in a classroom about contemporary issues can provide the teacher with numerous opportunities to further explore these issues while continuing to help students develop the critical-thinking skills so vital to the perpetuation of our political process. This twofold process is especially significant in view of the responsibility of social studies teachers to help educate the young to become active, involved, and informed citizens.

DEVELOPING CRITICAL-THINKING SKILLS

All of the following guidelines and activities for helping students develop critical-thinking skills and apply them to controversial issues are designed to promote an approach that emphasizes reason rather than emotionalism. The first step must be to develop and refine the skills required to separate fact from opinion. What, for example, is a statement of fact as opposed to a statement of opinion? How can the two be separated? Is there any value in separating them? How often does one speak, hear, or read statements of fact and statements of opinion? Can both kinds of statements be printed in a social studies textbook, announced on television or radio, or made by students, teachers, parents, and politicians?

Once the difference between fact and opinion has been established among the pronouncements issued by people representing the various sides of a controversial issue, the next step is to determine the points, if any, on which the two or more sides agree. What points are included by one side but omitted by the other? What points seem to have been neglected by all sides? What factors might account for such omissions?

When the points of agreement and omission have been determined, the points of disagreement should be noted. What could be the reasons for such disagreements? Which points of disagreement are based on statements of fact, and which are based on statements of opinion? Are the statements of opinion merely hypotheses or educated guesses, or are they generalizations based on the careful use of available data?

The study of history can help students examine contemporary issues, since most (if not all) contemporary issues have historical precedents. In dealing with a current social issue, students should consider what its precedents might be and whether they have been used as the basis of arguments or data presented about the issue. If historical precedents have been cited, are they truly analogous? Or, to reverse the question, students might be asked to consider what basic questions are raised by the contemporary issue. Have similar questions been raised about past issues? In regard to what kinds of situations? Were the issues resolved? If not, why not? If so, how were they resolved? Might the resolution

of a past issue have any bearing on how a current issue might best be resolved? In short, does the study of the past have any relevance for the
present? Might it have any relevance for the future if similar questions
continue to arise?

All of these questions lead to the last major step in the critical-
thinking process: having students review all the available data, arguments, and historical precedents about the issue under investigation, fo-
cusing on the uses of fact and opinion and the points of agreement, disagreement, and omission. Once the review has been completed, new generalizations
about the issue can be formed and supported by students. In helping students accomplish this task, the teacher should point out that a later presentation of new evidence may in turn cause these new generalizations to
be changed or revised.

To illustrate the critical-thinking process and allow students to
practice using critical-thinking skills, a teacher might wish to use the
three sample activities that appear on the following pages. Each activity
is self-contained to facilitate removal and reproduction.

Activity 1

DISTINGUISHING FACT FROM OPINION

A *fact* is something that is known with certainty. It has been proven to be valid or correct. A statement of fact could be "Christopher Columbus arrived in the Americas in 1492" or "George Washington's forces defeated the British troops at Yorktown in 1781."

An *opinion* is a belief that may or may not be based on facts. It is a conclusion held with some degree of confidence. A statement of opinion could be "Columbus was the greatest of all the European explorers" or "George Washington was the most famous military leader in all of American history."

Separating fact from opinion is a task that each of us faces every day. Imagine, for example, that you came across the following paragraph in the school newspaper:

> Our high school football team is great. This past season
> it won eight games. It lost only two games. In the eight
> games we won, we scored a total of 130 points. Our oppon-
> ents in those eight games scored a total of only 20 points.

In this example, the first sentence is a statement of *opinion*--that the football team is "great." This opinion is based on the following *facts*: that the team won eight of ten games, and that in those eight games the team scored 130 points to the opposition's 20.

Now, examine the following paragraphs and tell which sentences you think are *statements of opinion* and which sentences seem to be *statements of fact*. Identify each sentence by the letter that precedes it.

Paragraph 1

(a) Texas is a huge state. (b) In terms of size, it is 267,379 square miles in area. (c) Texas is the second-largest state in the United States. (d) Texas is about the size of all of New England plus New York State, Pennsylvania, Ohio, and Illinois. (e) Texas is larger in size than any country in Western Europe. (f) Texas has the friendli-est people in the world.

1. Which sentences in the paragraph are *statements of opinion?*
_____ Why?

2. Which sentences are *statements of fact?* _____
Why?

Paragraph 2

(a) Stephen F. Austin was a very successful *empresario*. (b) His colony began with 300 families consisting of 1,800 people. (c) By 1835 the Austin colony had grown to 1,500 families and 7,500 people. (d) No other Texas *empresario* had so many families settle a Mexican colonization grant. (e) Austin was the most popular of all the *empresarios*.

Questions

1. Which sentences above are *statements of opinion?* _____.
_____ Why?

2. Which ones are *statements of fact?* _____ Why?

Paragraph 3

(a) In 1836 all roads and trails in Texas were in very poor condition. (b) In those days people could go from place to place on foot, on horses, mules, or donkeys, or in wagons, carriages, or boats. (c) It usually took a whole day to ride 30 miles on a horse. (d) Most people did not like to travel outside the area where they lived.

Questions

1. Which sentences above are *statements of opinion?* _____
_____ Why?

2. Which sentences are *statements of fact?* _____
Why?

1. What is a "fact"?

2. What is an "opinion"?

3. Do you see any value in separating fact from opinion? Explain your answer.

4. Write a sentence that contains *both* a statement of opinion and a statement of fact.

17

Activity 2

IDENTIFYING CONFLICTING VIEWPOINTS

What can we do when we are confronted with two or more opinions or statements of fact that do not agree with one another? This problem occurs often in our daily lives, and especially in our political process.

Consider, for example, how you might resolve the conflicts of opinion or viewpoint in these two summaries of a school's football season.

Version 1

Our high school football team is great. This past season it won seven games and lost only three games. In the seven games we won, we scored a total of 130 points. Our opponents in those seven games scored a total of only 20 points.

Version 2

Our high school football team is not too good. This past season it lost three games and won seven. The games lost were the last three of the season. All were important district games. In those last three games we only scored a total of 6 points. Our opponents in those last three games scored a total of 90 points.

As you can see, the two students who wrote these versions have a difference of opinion about whether the high school football team is "great" or "not too good." If you needed to make a decision on the basis of two such conflicting descriptions, you might use the following steps in arriving at your own conclusion:

1. Determine the points on which the two versions *agree*.

2. Determine what points are made in one version but *omitted* in the other.

3. Determine the points on which the two versions *disagree*.

4. If the two versions disagree on a point, decide, on the basis of the available evidence, the probable cause or causes of the disagreement.

5. Determine how you could use both versions to reconstruct a third version.

Use the outline that follows to apply these five steps to the two descriptions of the high school football team.

1. Points of agreement:

2. Points omitted:
   a. Version 1 did not mention:

   b. Version 2 did not mention:

3. Points of disagreement:

4. Probable causes of the disagreement:

5. On a separate piece of paper, write a third version of your own that you think accurately describes the situation.

Activity 3

RESOLVING CONFLICTING VIEWPOINTS

In Activity 2 you considered five steps that can be used to resolve conflicting viewpoints. Now, keep those five steps in mind and apply them to these two very different versions of the causes of the Texas Revolution of 1836.

Version 1 (Texan view)

In March of 1836 many Texans declared their independence of Mexican rule. Those Texans had many good reasons for declaring their independence from Mexico.

Santa Anna had made himself the dictator of all of Mexico by forcing a legislature he controlled to grant him such power.

Although Santa Anna had promised the Texans more self-rule, he did not allow them to form a state separate from Coahuila.

In 1830 Santa Anna pushed through a law that prohibited other residents of the United

Version 2 (Mexican view)

In March of 1836 many Texans openly declared their independence of the Mexican government. Their action was wrong for several reasons.

As supreme ruler, Santa Anna had the right to take away whatever freedoms he pleased and rule as he thought best.

Santa Anna felt that to allow the Texans to have a separate state would make them too independent of Mexican rule. Besides, a supreme ruler has the right to change his mind about governmental matters.

Santa Anna believed that if immigration were not controlled there would be increasing pressure

States from moving to Texas. Many Texans feared that their population would dwindle.

Santa Anna had promised to use more soldiers to protect the colonists from hostile Indians. Instead of doing so, however, he actually encouraged some Indians to attack colonists who favored Texas independence. Santa Anna had also agreed to build new and better roads in Texas and provide better mail service, yet in 1836 the roads and mail service were as poor as ever.

In 1834 the Mexican government decided to stop issuing *empresario* land grants. The *empresarios* were the only people from whom settlers could get land in Mexico and Texas. The Mexican government appointed all *empresarios*. Many Texans felt that the *empresarios* would divide the land fairly. Otherwise, a few people could buy up the open lands and then set land prices higher than most colonists could afford to pay.

for more self-rule in Texas.

Santa Anna had many problems to solve, many of which he regarded as more important than providing more troops to protect Texans, building new roads in Texas, or improving the mail service in Texas. Besides, it was the responsibility of the Texans to protect themselves against Indian attacks. They were certainly capable of doing so.

In 1834 the Mexican government halted the *empresario* land-grant system in order to give Santa Anna more control over how the open lands in Texas were divided.

Summary Questions

1. What factors ahould be considered in attempting to resolve conflicts between two different stories or viewpoints?

2. Do you see any value in analyzing the differences between conflicting stories or viewpoints? Explain your answer.

3. What do you think responsible citizens should do when they are confronted with conflicting stories or viewpoints from politicians or other people--perhaps their friends?

4. On a separate piece of paper, write two conflicting versions, similar to the ones in this example, of one of the following topics:

   a. The causes of the American Revolution of 1776 or the Civil War of 1861.

   b. The institution of slavery.

   c. The actions of big businessmen in the United States during the late 19th century.

   d. The emergence of labor unions in the United States.

NOTES

1. For more information on this topic see Raymond H. Muessig, ed., *Controversial Issues in the Social Studies: A Contemporary Perspective*, 45th Yearbook of the National Council for the Social Studies, 1975.

2. James M. Benjamin, "What Have We Done to the Social Studies?," *Southwestern Journal of Social Education*, Spring-Summer 1974, p. 5.

3. Allan O. Kownslar, "What Should Be Done to the Social Studies?," *Southwestern Journal of Social Education*, Spring-Summer 1974, pp. 8-9.

4. Ibid., p. 9.

5. Benjamin, "What Have We Done?," pp. 5-6.

6. Kownslar, "What Should Be Done?," p. 9.

7. Ibid., p. 9.

8. Benjamin, "What Have We Done?," p. 6.

9. Kownslar, "What Should Be Done?," p. 11.

10. Benjamin, "What Have We Done?," p. 6.

11. Kownslar, "What Should Be Done?," p. 10.

12. See Richard S. Kirkendall, "The Status of History in the Schools," *Journal of American History*, September 1975, pp. 557-570.

13. Patricia Konstam, "The Textbook Battle," *Texas Observer*, November 4, 1977, p. 16.

14. As quoted in *Reader's Digest*, February 1978, p. 48.

15. Benjamin, "What Have We Done?," p. 6.

16. Kirkendall, "The Status of History," pp. 562-63.

17. Allan O. Kownslar, "The Status of History: Some Views and Suggestions," *Social Education*, October 1976, p. 448.

18. For more on this subject see Richard Brown, "A Note to the Teacher," in Allan O. Kownslar, *Discovering American History* (New York: Holt, Rinehart and Winston, 1969), p. xvi.

RESOURCES IN THE ERIC SYSTEM

This section describes some of the documents dealing with topics emphasized in this monograph which have been entered into the ERIC system. Each document is identified by a six-digit number. EJ numbers indicate journal articles; ED numbers are used for other kinds of documents.

If you want to read a document with an ED number, check to see whether your local library or instructional media center subscribes to the ERIC microfiche collection. (For a list of libraries in your area that subscribe to the ERIC system, write to ERIC/ChESS, 855 Broadway, Boulder, Colorado 80302.)

If an ERIC collection is not easily accessible, or if you want a personal copy of an ED document in either microfiche (MF) or hard copy (HC), write to ERIC Document Reproduction Services (EDRS), Computer Microfilm International Corporation, P.O. Box 190, Arlington, Virginia. All orders must be accompanied by payment in full, plus postage. Prices cited for each ED document are correct as of June 1, 1978. Documents not available from EDRS can usually be ordered from the publisher.

If your local library does not have a journal article that you want, you may write for one or more reprints to University Microfilms, 300 North Zeeb Road, Ann Arbor, Michigan 48106. The following information is needed: title of periodical or journal, title of article, author, date of issue, volume number, and number of pages to be copied. A single reprint costs $6.00; there is a $1.00 charge for each additional reprint. All orders must be accompanied by payment in full, plus postage.

American Civilization in Historic Perspective. Part I: A Guide for Teaching Social Studies, Grade 11. Albany, New York: New York State Education Department, 1970. ED 065 385. Not available from EDRS; order from Publications Distribution Unit, Finance Section, State Education Department, Albany, New York 12224 (217 pp., $1.00).

This teaching guide offers illustrative and reference materials about three topics: mass media, conflicting ideologies, and social control. The emphasis is on organizing the selections as short cases or studies. Related understandings are grouped together to emphasize this approach. The inductive method encourages students to examine the presentations objectively, analyze and interpret them in terms of the medium, and consider the historic development of the issues.

Banks, James A. "Teaching Strategies for Discussion of Justice in America: Fact or Fiction?" *Social Education* 7, no. 37 (November 1973), pp. 639-642. EJ 086 970.

Several key generalizations which students can derive about the legal status of ethnic minorities in the United States are identified in this article, as are major events, treaties, and court cases essential for understanding the struggle for justice among nonwhites.

Connecticut Council for the Social Studies. *The U.S. Constitution and Its Development*. New Haven: Yale University, 1976. ED 137 161. EDRS Price: MF $0.83, HC $3.50; plus postage (70 pp).

This report consists of eight articles on constitutional issues derived from papers presented at a 1976 social studies conference. It is intended to be used by teachers in planning and implementing curriculum materials on the U.S. Constitution. The first article discusses interpretive problems in the formation of the Constitution and gives examples of how historiographic issues can be effectively used in the teaching of history. The second article explores ways of teaching and understanding legal terms, reasoning, analysis, and rules. In the third article, the English roots of American constitutionalism are explored. A discussion of women's rights under the Constitution is found in the fourth article. Urban problems before the courts, particularly ways in which social studies teachers can draw themes from court action, are discussed in the fifth article. The sixth article presents a history of the Supreme Court's handling of cases related to education. The seventh article contains a report of recent trends of freedom of expression in American constitutional law. The final article compares myths, opinions, and facts about the U.S. Constitution with those of the constitution of the Union of Soviet Socialist Republics.

Gomez, Rudolph, et al., eds. *The Social Reality of Ethnic America.*
Lexington, Massachusetts: D.C. Heath and Co., 1974. ED 097 384.
Not available from EDRS; order from D.C. Heath and Co., 125 Spring
Street, Lexington, Massachusetts 02173 (412 pp., $5.95).

Each of the four parts of this book deals with problems and issues
related to the history of an ethnic group in the United States.
Black Americans, American Indians, Japanese Americans, and Mexican
Americans were the groups chosen for the study.

Hogeboom, Willard L. "The Case for Labor Studies in the Curriculum."
Social Science Record 23, no. 1 (February 1975), pp. 4-6. EJ 140 334.

The author of this article argues that labor studies should be a
fundamental part of the social studies curriculum. A bibliography
of labor studies materials and resources for teachers is included.

Life, Liberty, and the Pursuit of Happiness. Materials for Using American
Issues Forum in the American History Classroom, Topic 9. Albany,
New York: New York State Education Department, 1976. ED 129 661.
EDRS price: MF $0.83, HC $2.06; plus postage (35 pp.).

This document provides four modules of classroom strategies for
examing U.S. history in the context of contemporary issues. "The
Right to Life" uses the Karen Anne Quinlan case as a model for ex-
ploring moral, legal, and medical issues related to euthanasia. Students discuss the reasoning and viewpoints of various groups associated with the case and consider the merits of a "living will." "The
Dream of Success" focuses on problems involved in making a career
choice and allows students to critically analyze strengths and
weaknesses of a variety of work roles. Self-evaluation instruments
and interviews with workers help students identify factors influ-
encing people to be satisfied or dissatisfied with their jobs.
"The Pursuit of Pleasure" employs an inquiry strategy to analyze
evidence and formulate conclusions about leisure in American society.
In "The Fruits of Wisdom," students learn and apply a problem-solv-
ing technique to assess the social and economic impact of the Alaska

pipeline. Rationales and teaching plans are provided for all modules, which are being field-tested.

Merrill, Charles. "Time and the Teacher." *History Teacher* 5, no. 2 (January 1972), pp. 42-47. EJ 049 614.

The author of this article believes that teachers must help students understand that today's events and social conditions will be tomorrow's history. Presenting contemporary social problems in relation to past events, he argues, will enable students to perceive history more clearly and cope better with their own world.

"Rx Education: Back to Basics (Sort Of)." *Science News*, June 1976. EJ 143 602.

This article presents a tentative prescription for remedying academic deficiencies related to knowledge of the world and fundamental life skills. The authors recommend that more emphasis be placed in the schools on skills required for simple computation, solving consumer problems, coherence, and idea development.

Schofield, Dee. *Issues in Basic Education*. NAESP School Leadership Digest Second Series, no. 12; ERIC/CEM Research Analysis Series, no. 27. Washington, D.C.: National Association of Elementary School Principals and ERIC Clearinghouse on Educational Management, 1976. ED 128 873. EDRS price: MF $0.83, HC $2.06; plus postage (31 pp.). Also available from NAESP, 1801 North Moore Street, Arlington, Virginia 22209 ($1.50).

This booklet describes the back-to-basics movement as resulting from public alarm over the increase in functional illiteracy—students' inability to solve everyday problems requiring basic language and mathematics skills. Back-to-basics schools are growing in popularity, though many educators are critical of what they consider to be the regressive tendencies of fundamentalist education. The author summarizes the thinking of theorists, such as Alfred North Whitehead, who suggest that language and mathematic skills, as traditionally defined, do not constitute the true basics of education. Instead, the cognitive, affective, and developmental skills necessary for mature and effective communication are the proper educational goals. The author concludes that it would be regrettable if the pressing problem of illiteracy became rigidly linked with fundamentalist conservatism.

Shaver, James P. "The Bicentennial and the Analysis of Public Issues." Paper presented at the annual meeting of the Alabama State Council for the Social Studies, Tuscaloosa, Alabama, November 1, 1975. ED 115 569. EDRS price: MF $0.83, HC $1.67; plus postage (7 pp.).

The author of this paper presents some ways of making discussions of issues provided by the American Issues Forum meaningful to students and applicable to decision making outside the classroom. He points out that treatment of the issues raised during the founding of the nation and during consideration of public policy since then must take into account the conflicting values inherent in a democratic society.

United States History in the Secondary School: The American Mind. Point Pleasant Beach, New Jersey: Point Pleasant Beach Board of Education, 1968. ED 045 496. EDRS price: MF $0.83, HC $3.50; plus postage (60 pp.).

The emphasis of the unit is on values held by Americans rather than on social and economic forces. The material shows the maturing of the American mind, from the Puritan experiment during our Colonial period through the conflicts of the 20th century. Among its specific objectives are to help students (1) identify uniquely American patterns of thought, (2) understand that a free society breeds conflict of ideas and that democracy provides an avenue for resolution, (3) realize the role of the individual in forming public opinion, and (4) create their own philosophy of life, taking into consideration the ideas and rights of others.

II. FOUR SAMPLE LESSONS

HOW TO USE THESE LESSONS

The steps involved in each of the three introductory activities provided at the end of Part I can be applied to the four lessons which follow. Each of the four focuses on a modern-day controversial issue. Included in the presentation of each issue are statements of both fact and opinion, points of both agreement and disagreement, and significant omissions by one side or the other. A critical examination of these lessons can help students continue to develop their critical-thinking skills as well as clarify some of their personal values in regard to contemporary and, for the most part, emotion-laden issues.

The first lesson is about the Allan Bakke case, which was decided by the U.S. Supreme Court on June 28, 1978. The second lesson deals with the proposed Equal Rights Amendment. The third lesson elaborates on the role of political patronage and the David Marston issue of 1976-1978. The last lesson concerns recent First Amendment freedoms exercised by the American Nazi party.

Each lesson is presented in two sections. The first section contains suggestions for classroom treatment of the issue. The second part consists of materials for student use.

Teachers should note that any of the four lessons can easily be used to introduce whatever issues may be the subjects of tomorrow's headlines. Although the controversy surrounding a contemporary social issue may fade away after its legal resolution, similar debates related to the same basic questions will probably arise in the future. Morever, as the background material provided for each lesson shows, all the basic issues that underlie the specific subjects of these four lessons have been the focus of similar controversies in the past. Thus, an examination of these issues can provide students with the skills and insights needed to form and revise hypotheses and generalizations about past, present, and future history.

LESSON 1: THE ALLAN BAKKE CASE

By Theresa Arocha, Jessie Gunn, Tim Malone, and Mack Pryor

Overview

This lesson contains the following student materials:

Assignment 1 (Parts 1-4). Fictional accounts that raise questions about the validity or justification of the use of quota systems and other forms of discrimination.

Assignment 2. A summary of the Allan Bakke case, including the reasons for his suit against the School of Medicine at the University of California at Davis.

Assignment 3. Sample pros and cons on the merits of the Bakke case.

Assignment 4. A fictional play that again raises the question of when a quota system or reverse discrimination may be justified.

Lesson Objectives

Students will be able to *recognize problems for inquiry* (Is use of a quota system or reverse discrimination ever justifiable? How equal should opportunities be for our citizens?) and *offer hypotheses* in response to these questions after discussing one or more parts of Assignment 1. *Testing the validity of the hypotheses* will occur as the students examine material in Assignments 2, 3, and 4. Finally, after evaluating the material presented in Assignment 4, students should be able to *form and support generalizations* about the worth of quota systems or reverse discrimination and about the extent to which certain opportunities should be made equal for our citizens.

Intended Student Audience: Grades 9-12.

Suggested Time for Classroom Use of Materials: Three to five class periods.

Specific Objectives

Cognitive Objectives. Upon completion of this lesson students will:

knowledge goals	1.	Be able to explain what "reverse discrimination" implies or signifies to many Americans.
	2.	Know what questions were raised by the Allan Bakke case about the possible good and bad results of establishing quota systems or goals for professional schools.

skill development	3. Be able to read, compare, interpret, and acquire information about the Bakke case and about similar instances of the use of quota systems to combat discrimination.
	4. Recognize these central problems for inquiry: How equal should a variety of opportunities be for all of our citizens? When is a quota system or reverse discrimination ever justifiable?
	5. Be able to form hypotheses in response to the central questions for inquiry.
	6. Be able to form and support generalizations about whether educational and other kinds of opportunities should be made equal for all citizens and whether a quota system or reverse discrimination is ever justifiable.

Affective Objectives. Upon completion of this lesson students will:

empathy	1. Understand and be able to explain the views of both those who favor and those who are opposed to the practice of using quota systems or reverse discrimination.
social participation	2. Be willing to participate in group discussions to examine information about the Bakke case.
values clarification	3. Be willing to attempt to analyze objectively both their own values and those held by others in regard to the use of quota systems and reverse discrimination.
tolerance	4. Be willing to tolerate (but not necessarily agree with) a variety of conflicting viewpoints on a controversial topic.

Teaching Suggestions

Introducing the Lesson

This lesson can be introduced in at least two different ways. One way would be to ask all the students to consider each of the four fictional accounts in Assignment 1. Another way would be to divide the class into eight groups and assign two groups to examine each of the four parts.

If group work is used, you may want to ensure that all groups contain representative proportions of what you regard as below-average, average, and above-average students. Each group should be allowed to select a leader. When all the groups have completed their examinations of the assignments, each leader should be prepared to report the findings of the group. This report should address the following question, which should be written on the chalkboard before the students begin the assignment: "Suppose you had to give your part of Assignment 1 a title worded as an abstract question. What would your question be?" Emphasize that in phrasing their questions students should not use proper names or personal pronouns. Also stress that while trying out possible questions, all group members should feel free to express their ideas and suggestions.

As additional preparation for this assignment, you might want to have the class review Activity 3, supplied in Part I of this volume. Ask students to reword the title of that particular lesson--"Resolving Conflicting Viewpoints"--as a question. Point out that nowhere in the title can one find the words "high school," "football team," "won," or "lost," and that the title is a general, rather than specific, reference to the issue involved, which in this case happens to be the win-lose record of a high school football team. Ask what abstract questions could have been used as titles for the other two activities in Part I. (Some responses might be "What makes two views on the same subject differ?," "How many sides can a story have?," or even such value-laden questions as "Is winning all that counts?" and "Is greatness all that counts?")

Once the students have formulated their abstract title questions,

record them on the chalkboard. If the students have been working in
groups, ask the entire class to look for similarities and differences
in the questions submitted by various groups. If there are differences
ask the students to consider which questions best represent the issues
raised in each situation. If they have not already been suggested in
some form, read aloud the central problems for inquiry identified for
this lesson. (How equal should opportunities be for all our citizens?
When, if ever, is a quota system or reverse discrimination justifiable?).
Ask if these questions accurately summarize the questions formulated by
the students. Then ask the class to suggest answers to them. Ask what
"opportunities" might be considered. What might "equal" mean? Could
it mean what Abraham Lincoln said when he wrote:

"I think the authors [of the Declaration of Independence] intended
to include all men, but they did not intend to declare all men equal in
all respects. They did not mean to say all were equal in color, size,
intellect, moral development, or social capacity. They defined with
tolerable distinctness in what respects they did consider all men created
equal--equal in certain unalienable rights, among which are life, liberty,
and the pursuit of happiness. This they said, and this they meant."

Continue the discussion by asking: What is a "quota system"? How
might it function? What is "discrimination"? Did any of the situations
in Assignment 1 seem to have anything to do with equality, a quota system,
or reverse discrimination? Could using a quota system or reverse discrimination in our present-day society ever be justifiable? If so, how and
why? If not, why not? Once responses to these questions have been
discussed, tell the students that their answers will be used as major
points for consideration as they go on to examine information about the
Allan Bakke case.

You may want to make a record of students' questions and responses
for later use in student research projects as well as in further activities related to the controversy surrounding the Bakke case. The same
procedure can be followed in presenting the other three lessons.

Continuing the Lesson

Assignment 2 contains a summary of the Allan Bakke case, including
the reasons for Bakke's successful suit against the medical school at the

University of California at Davis.

This summary should be duplicated and given to students. After students have read this material, devote a class period to discussing the three questions that accompany the assignment. This procedure will allow all the students to become familiar with the reasons why Bakke instituted his suit, the initial responses to it, the main characters involved, and the final outcome of the case. During this discussion, make sure that the students consider what roles "equality," a "quota system," and "reverse discrimination" seemed to play in the case. What other factors might have played a part? What was the basis for the ultimate decision of the court? By this time the class should be ready to take a closer look at the sample pro and con arguments presented in Assignment 3. Additional summaries of the opinions offered by the Supreme Court justices in the Bakke case can also be examined in the July 10, 1978, issue of *Newsweek*.

When students examine the arguments presented in Assignment 3, they should identify reasons for making judgments about which ones seem to have the most merit or to be the most reasonable. You may wish to make a list of these criteria for later reconsideration and future reference. Ask the class to suggest other pros and cons that might have been included in the sample list.

Conclude the discussion of Assignment 3 by having the students consider how any of the arguments associated with the Bakke case could be used in support of or in opposition to the premise that all citizens should have equal educational opportunities. Does there seem to be one clear-cut answer, or are there several answers? Ask students to define the words "dilemma" and "controversial." Could their definitions apply in any way to questions raised by the Bakke case?

After thoroughly discussing the Bakke case, introduce Assignment 4, a fictional play about a comparable high school situation. After the entire class has read the introduction, you may want to let student volunteers act out the parts of Mrs. Jenkins, Doris, Fred, Richard, and Mr. Hyde. The discussion afterward should focus on how the terms "equality," "quota system," and "reverse discrimination" might be applied to the situations and problems dramatized in the play. Are the words "dilemma" and "controversial" also applicable? Conclude the discussion by asking students to write a paragraph enlarging upon the following topic sentence, supporting their arguments with reasons and examples: "A quota system and forms of reverse discrimination (are never/are sometimes/ are) justifiable in our society as we attempt to provide equality for all of our citizens."

Optional Teaching Strategies

If you decide to use this lesson early in the school year, students could further expand and evaluate their responses if it were used in conjunction with an examination of one or more of the following issues in U.S. history:

1. Acts of discrimination by the Puritans against non-Puritans in colonial Massachusetts.

2. Suffrage discrimination policies against nonproperty holders prior to 1824.

3. Acts of discrimination against black slaves prior to the adoption of the 13th-15th amendments.

4. The advent of Jim Crowism from 1876 to 1954.

5. Immigration quota systems from the 1880s to 1964.

6. Controversies over the busing of public school students from 1964 to the present.

7. Suffrage discrimination policies restricting the political actions of women until the passage of the 19th Amendment.

8. Hiring practices affecting women and minority groups since 1942.

9. The *Baker vs. Carr* Supreme Court decision.

10. Quota systems adopted by the Democratic party in 1972 for choosing delegates to national conventions.

11. The reasons for and possible long-range results of the *Brown vs. Topeka* Supreme Court decision.

Additional Reading

Books and Magazine Articles

Brill, Stephen A. "The Court's Bakke Spasms." *Esquire,* April 11, 1978, p. 17.

Bundy, McGeorge. "The Issue Before the Court: Who Gets Ahead in America?" *Atlantic,* November 1977, pp. 41-50.

Chase, H.W., and Ducat, C.R. *Supplement to Constitutional Interpretation, 1977: "Bakke vs. Regents of the University of California."* St. Paul: West Publishing Co., 1977.

Connolly, Paul H. "The Bakke Case: The Courts vs. Self-Governments." *National Review,* October 28, 1977, pp. 1225-28.

Cousins, Norman. "The Bakke Case: Just the Beginning." *Saturday Review,* November 26, 1977, p. 4.

Footlick, Jerrold. "Bakke Battle." *Newsweek,* October 24, 1977, pp. 45-46.

Footlick, Jerrold. "The Bakke Brief." *Newsweek,* September 19, 1977, p. 97.

Footlick, Jerrold. "The Furor Over Reverse Discrimination." *Newsweek,* September 26, 1977, pp. 52-55.

Gross, Barry R. *Reverse Discrimination.* Buffalo: Prometheus Books, 1977.

"Hard Cases Coming, The." *Newsweek,* July 10, 1978, p. 32.

Lawrence, Charles, III. "The Bakke Case: Are Racial Quotas Defensible?" *Saturday Review,* October 15, 1977, p. 16.

Shrum, Robert. "Racist Tests: The Hidden Issue of Bakke." *New Times,* February 6, 1978.

Walsh, J. "Bakke Case: Question of Special Minority Admission Programs." *Science,* July 1, 1977, pp. 25-27.

"Year Ahead, The: Bakke Case Looms on the Supreme Court's Dockets." *American Bar Association Journal,* November 1977, pp. 1551-54.

Newspapers

Many local and national newspapers periodically print articles that are helpful to both students and teachers. The following resources are useful.

Wall Street Journal. Between August 23, 1977, and October 13, 1977, the *Journal* printed a number of editorials and follow-up articles that students would find helpful. The availability of these issues will depend upon local library resources.

New York Times. Most coverage occurred between August and November 1977. The *Times* is available in most high school libraries. Many local newspapers carried syndicated reprints of these articles.

Christian Science Monitor. The *Monitor* began a series of articles in July 1977 which were focused primarily on the ethical questions. Many issues between July and November 1977 contain enlightening material.

STUDENT MATERIALS FOR LESSON 1

Lesson 1, Assignment 1

WHAT IS FAIR?   FOUR EVERYDAY DILEMMAS

Part 1

Read the material below and answer the questions that follow.

"When I was a kid, I took the bus to school. We had an informal rule that you boarded the bus in the order that you arrived at the bus stop. I suppose the rule was originally meant to keep big kids from bullying their way onto the bus first.

"Jimmy was a little boy who lived right next to the bus stop. It was very important to him that he be the first one on the bus. Each morning he'd get up very early and rush to dress and eat his breakfast so that he'd arrive before the rest of us.

"One day, after several years of this, some of us decided to change the rule. The new rule was that we would get on the bus in order of size, with the smallest kids getting on first. The bus had become crowded, and we thought the smallest kids most needed a seat.

"Jimmy was angry that he could no longer get a seat. He felt that he had worked hard at learning how to be best in the old system and that the new rule was designed to cheat him out of his rightfully earned spot. He couldn't help it if he was now one of the bigger kids, he argued. Why should his size be used against him?

"I had a hard time taking Jimmy's arguments seriously. The new rule seemed to be what we needed for the time being. It didn't really hurt us big kids to stand during the ride to school. Besides, Jimmy had been sitting for a long time."

Questions

1. Do you think that using size as a basis for awarding special privileges is ever justifiable? Give reasons for your answer.

2.   Do you think that awarding privileges on a first-come first-served basis is ever justifiable?   Explain your answer.

3.   Because Jimmy lives closest to the bus stop, he has a better chance to be first in line.   Is this fair?   Explain your reasoning.

4.   In this story, who changed the rule?   Why?

5.   In this situation, do you think Jimmy should obey a rule he doesn't agree with?   Explain your answer.

6.   Suggest a compromise between Jimmy's position and that of other kids who ride the bus.   What would be the basis for your compromise?

The narrative in this lesson was taken from Charles Lawrence III, "The Bakke Case: Are Racial Quotas Defensible?," *Saturday Review,* October 15, 1977, p. 16.

Part 2

Think about the following situations and answer the questions.

Situation 1: If I burn down your home, do I owe you something?

Situation 2: If my father burns down your home, do I owe you something?

Situation 3: If a group of which I am a member burns down your home, do I owe you something?

Questions

1. What differences are there between situations 1, 2, and 3?

2. In which situation or situations might I owe you something? Why?

3. If I do owe you something, how could I repay you? Who should decide this?

4. If I am not directly responsible for situation 3, could I be held indirectly responsible if I had not tried to prevent others in my group from taking this action?

Part 3

Read the story below and answer the questions that follow.

Mrs. Smith has given her sophomore class an essay exam during fourth period. George, a rather weak student, has placed his paper on the bottom of the stack. During Mrs. Smith's lunch break, he sneaks into the room and looks over his paper, correcting some spelling mistakes, adding a few good vocabulary words, and recopying a page or two for good measure. While he is replacing his paper--this time in the middle of the stack, so as not to create suspicion--he turns over all of the papers, and Tim's exam falls into the wastebasket, unnoticed.

When all the exams have been graded, Mrs. Smith makes two surprising discoveries: (1) George's paper has very few errors, and he receives a grade of 89; (2) Tim, one of the best students in the class, apparently did not turn in a paper at all. When confronted with this accusation, Tim claims to have taken the exam and is angry that Mrs. Smith has mis-placed his paper. Mrs. Smith honestly does not remember whether Tim turned in a paper or not--but the fact is that his paper is not there.

In the middle of the discussion about the problem, Mr. Estes, the janitor, walks in and tells Mrs. Smith that he saw George in the room during lunch, thumbing through the test papers. George confesses and receives an "F" on the exam. Mrs. Smith tells Tim that he must take the exam over. Tim feels that he has been unfairly treated. He offers to compromise by accepting George's score of 89. Mrs. Smith refuses and demands that Tim take the test over, regardless of whose fault the problem is.

Questions

1. Do you think that Tim should have the right to retake the exam? Explain.

2. Do you think that Mrs. Smith should require Tim to redo the paper? Explain.

3. If Tim takes the test over, should he be graded the same as all the other students who took the exam? Or should he be given some extra credit to compensate for his misfortune? Explain.

4. Does George owe Tim anything for causing the disaster?

5. How would you handle the situation if you were the teacher in this story? Why?

Part 4

Read the story below and answer the questions that follow.

As you walk into Memorial High School one morning, you and all the other students are handed the following memorandum:

"The administration wishes to announce that from this day on all students will be seated in classrooms in reverse alphabetical order. This order will prevail in class roll taking, student-assembly seating, lines, and class registrations. Hereafter, students whose names begin with Z, Y, and X will be first in line, and the Cs, Bs, and As will be last. This arrangement will continue until further notice."

Although the students whose last names were Adams, Baker, and Carter were not happy about the new rule, they could understand the need to share the "first choices" with students who had always been last in line. The real conflict came, however, when Carole Baker found that she would not get to take turns sitting in the front row. Bill Watson explained that according to the administration ruling, he and Bob Zimmerman would always be first--at least until some future announcement.

Carole complained that this was not fair. She argued that taking turns and sharing was the fair way, the democratic way, the American way. Although she was sorry that Bill and Bob had been relegated to the back-row seats in the past, she had not been responsible for that tradition--yet now she was to be penalized for it. "That simply is not fair," said Carole.

Bill and Bob reminded Carole that they had been last in line for everything--class roll taking, P.E. locker assignments, cafeteria lines, even the grading of tests and notebooks. "Now you must be last for a long time so that we can feel good about being first for a while," Bob told her. "*Then* we can talk about sharing the choice positions."

There seemed to be no way to simultaneously please students at both ends of the alphabet.

Questions

1. How have the students whose names begin with W or Z been hurt by their positions "at the end of every line"? Suppose your last name was Zinkus in this situation; can you imagine how you would feel?

2. Do you think that simply turning around the traditional alphabetical order is the best way to give everyone a turn at being first? Will doing this compensate the Xs, Ys, and Zs for the unfair treatment they used to receive?

3. Can you think of any way of dealing with this situation which would allow everyone to feel fairly treated? Explain how you would resolve the problem.

PEOPLE AND ISSUES IN THE BAKKE CASE

After reading about the issues and characters involved in the Bakke case, answer the questions that follow the material.

Background

Allan Bakke, in 1973, was a white male engineer who had twice been denied admission to the School of Medicine at the University of California at Davis. The university then had a special admissions program that set aside 16 of every 100 enrollment spots for disadvantaged minority students. The purpose of this policy was to "equalize" opportunities for students.

Even though Bakke did not apply under the special admissions program, he contended that he had been a victim of reverse discrimination because the 16 minority students admitted under the program were less qualified than he; thus, he charged, he had been denied admission solely because of his race. It was true that some of the people admitted under the special admissions program had both lower grade-point averages and substantially lower scores on the Medical College Aptitude Test than Bakke. However, advocates of the special program claimed that the evaluation criteria were not valid, and that the need for doctors of various minority groups was so urgent that the usual admission standards should not be binding.

Claiming reverse discrimination, Bakke sued the California medical school. He fought the issue in local and state courts and finally, in 1977, took his case to the U.S. Supreme Court and won.

Major Characters

Allan Bakke. The plaintiff. White male, currently 37 years old. Applied for admission in 1973 and 1974 to the School of Medicine at the University of California at Davis (at that time he was 32). Graduated from the University of Minnesota in 1962 with a B.S. in Mechanical Engineering. Attended graduate school at the University of Minnesota 1962-63. Served as an officer in the U.S. Marine Corps, 1963-67; worked as a research engineer for NASA after discharge; did graduate work at Stanford University in mechanical engineering and received his M.S. in 1970.

   George Lowry, M.D. Associate dean of student affairs and chairman of the admissions committee, University of California at Davis medical school.

   Peter Storandt. Assistant to Dr. Lowry. Became leading name in case because of his correspondence with Bakke in which the current lawsuit was discussed.

   Archibald Cox. Counsel for the university, former Watergate prosecutor. Assisted in defense by Paul J. Mishkin and Gary Morrison.

Questions

1. Who is Allan Bakke? Why did he sue the medical school?

2. How did advocates of the special admissions program respond to Bakke's charge?

3. Identify (a) George Lowry, (b) Peter Storandt, (c) Archibald Cox.

Lesson 1, Assignment 3

ARGUMENTS FOR AND AGAINST BAKKE'S POSITION

The Bakke case provoked a great deal of discussion and debate. Some of the pro and con arguments are summarized below. Read them carefully and think about which ones seem to have the most merit; then answer the questions that follow.

Arguments opposed to Bakke

Educational opportunities for many minority groups have been inferior. Comparing the test scores and grade-point averages of minorities and whites does not necessarily give an accurate indication of their relative abilities. It could be argued that a minority student with a GPA of 2.9 has shown more potential than a white with a GPA of 3.1.

The fact that members of minorities are underrepresented in such professions as medicine reinforces racial prejudice and is destructive to the self-esteem of minority members. There are enough minority members with respectable qualifications so that this program, even if carried out on a national scale,

Arguments in support of Bakke

No doubt this could happen; however, it would also be possible to find cases where the reverse was true. There is no reason why the admissions committee should not consider hardship cases and relative achievement of individuals without regard for race. In fact, in 1973, the special program was nominally for *all* disadvantaged applicants regardless of race.. In practice, however, whites who applied under the program were not even considered.

High professional status does not necessarily protect minorities from bigotry; it may even, in fact, exacerbate it because it adds the element of envy. This sort of program will be regarded by many as proof that members of minorities are unable to compete on equal terms with whites. What will be the effect on the self-

could not substantially affect the quality of medical care.

A quota system is legitimate because it is the only way to ensure prevention of discrimination on racial grounds.

The California medical school system has an obligation to train professionals from minority groups to provide for the medical needs of minority communities.

To rule in favor of Bakke would promote and endorse the tendency of graduate and professional schools to be white enclaves.

esteem of a person who is given official notice that he or she is to be the recipient of an undeserved charitable gesture?

A quota system that reserves a percentage of admissions for any particular group in society violates the spirit of our Constitution and our "equal opportunity" laws.

Federal laws forbid any discrimination on the basis of race. Besides, professionals are professionals, no matter to what race they belong. White doctors can serve black communities just as capably as black doctors can serve white communities.

People should be admitted to professional schools solely on the basis of individual performance and merit, as measured by entrance tests, grades, and recommendations.

Questions

1. Do you see any legal reasons why Bakke should have been admitted to the medical school? Explain.

2. Do you see any reasons why some entrance requirements of professional schools should be waived or lowered for minority groups? Explain.

3. How would you have decided the Bakke case? Why?

4. How would you now answer the question "How 'equal' should educational opportunities be for all of our citizens?" What reasons can you give for your answer?

Lesson 1, Assignment 4

APPLYING YOUR THOUGHTS ABOUT THE CASE

The first three assignments required you to consider the extent to which educational opportunities should be made equal for citizens of this country. This issue was presented in the context of the Bakke case.

In this lesson you will need to think about how you would apply your views on the matter to the imaginary situation described in the play that follows. After you read the play, you will be asked to answer questions about it.

The setting for the play is Jefferson High School, which is located in a small town (Anston) close to a large city. In recent years, housing developments inhabited by people working in the city have been built in the school district.

Currently, about 70 percent of the students at Jefferson are from Anston or surrounding rural areas. The parents of many of these students also attended Jefferson. Most of the teachers are from the small town, as are six of the seven members of the school board. Jefferson could thus be described as a rural school with solid, long-standing traditions.

The students from the housing developments feel at a disadvantage. Unlike the majority of the students, they are new arrivals. Their parents had not known one another previously or achieved social standing in the community. Few of the new students are interested in the established acitvities of the high school, such as the Rodeo Club and the Farmers' Coop. The new students also have the feeling, perhaps justified, that they would not be entirely welcome if they tried to join such clubs.

The relationship between the two student groups is characterized at best by friendly rivalry, at worst by open contempt and hostility. Students from the small town and the country area are known as "the Boots," those from the subdivisions as "the Beads." However it is not unknown for them to be called "the Hicks" and "the Freaks," respectively.

The biggest project at Jefferson is the preparation of the school yearbook. Much labor and expense is expended in the effort, and the school and the community are justifiably proud of the book's quality.

Competition for places on the staff is such that there are several times as many applicants as there are places. Not only does serving on the yearbook staff carry high prestige, it virtually assures a good recommendation when a student applies for college or a job. Applicants for the staff are screened by a committee consisting of the three senior staff members, the faculty adviser, and the principal. Applicants are required to submit their grade records in English and journalism. They are also given and graded on a sample assignment appropriate to the position they have applied for. The committee uses these data to select the applicants.

This year the committee consists of Doris and Fred, who live in the small town, and Richard, one of the few Beads to have served on the annual staff. The adviser is Mrs. Jenkins, who is from out of state and has been teaching at Jefferson for three years. Mr. Hyde, the principal, is a native of Anston.

As the scene opens, the committee is seated around a conference table. They have decided who are to fill all the positions but one.

MRS. JENKINS: Well, that leaves the activities editor to decide upon. What have you got on that, Doris?

DORIS: I have interviewed seven applicants, and two seemed pretty good. I had them write up and photograph the stock show. They were Paul Morris (heads nod in recognition) and Jerry Marshall.

FRED: Jerry transferred in last year, didn't he?

RICHARD: You mean he's a Bead, don't you?

DORIS: That's neither here nor there. I made copies of their stories and vital statistics, and here are the pictures they took.

(Doris hands out the pictures and stories, which members study for a few minutes, passing the photographs around.)

FRED: Where did Jerry get his camera, out of a gum machine?

RICHARD: Just about. He can't lay out the money for an expensive one like Paul has.

(The committee studies the material for a few minutes longer.)

MRS. JENKINS: There really doesn't seem to be much doubt in this case. I figure Marshall's GPA at 3.25 and Morris's at 3.75. Aside from the photos, and we do pride ourselves in the quality of our photography, there are some pretty gross mistakes in Marshall's story.

FRED: Yeah, listen to this: "The prize steer was a fine bull shown by. . . ."

(All but Richard show signs of amusement.)

RICHARD: I don't think the assignment was fair. Jerry is from Pittsburgh. On the first try any hayseed could beat him on a stock show story.

FRED: Maybe next time he'll include the steer's milk production.

RICHARD: I don't think that Paul and his bunch could cover the janitor replacing a light bulb.

FRED: By "his bunch" you mean. . . .

MR. HYDE: We are getting off the subject. Doris, you conducted the interviews. What are your thoughts?

DORIS: Well, we all know Paul. Jerry seems all right, but it is sort of hard to tell when you first meet someone. (She pauses.) Something else occurred to me. Maybe we ought to have more . . . oh, variety in our annual staff.

MR. HYDE: What do you mean?

DORIS: You know, if we had people with different interests . . . backgrounds. You know.

MRS. JENKINS: She means more Beads.

MR. HYDE: Oh, no! Not that can of worms again.

RICHARD: I'm with Doris. It's about time we got our fair share.

DORIS: That's sort of what I was thinking. If more Beads got on the yearbook staff and Student Council and all, they might be more friendly . . . (Richard frowns and starts to say something. Doris hurriedly goes on.) . . . and the rest of us might think better of them and not call them Freaks.

(The listeners look uncomfortable when the last word is spoken. It is not used in polite company or conversation.)

FRED: Doris, you just finished saying that whether someone was a Boot or a Bead was neither here nor there. I agree. There is only one fair way to do this--decide who will get the job the same way we decided on the other positions today, the way it's been done in the past.

RICHARD: Like they used to choose the Homecoming queen?

(Fred, Doris, and Mr. Hyde show signs of embarrassment. Formerly, there had been a rule that only girls whose mothers were Jefferson graduates were eligible to be elected Homecoming queen.)

MR. HYDE: I won't deny that there were instances of unfairness in the past, but I think we have cleared them up. You will have to admit that I have always been ready to listen to complaints. It seems as though I spend half my time listening to one side or the other.

(Richard obviously wants to say something but is reluctant.)

MR. HYDE: (Sharply.) Come on, if you know of some instance of unfairness, let's hear about it.

RICHARD: I've heard some Beads say that teachers from Anston were partial to Boots.

MRS. JENKINS: I hear a million excuses for poor performance. That one falls somewhere between a low biorhythm and a bad horoscope.

DORIS: About a third of the students are Beads. But when I look at the honor roll, it seem that less than one-fourth of the names are Beads.

RICHARD: It's tough to transfer into a new school. You have to get used

to new textbooks, different methods of teaching. None of us is
interested in agriculture courses.

MRS. JENKINS: We can hardly have 20 or 30 separate 11th-grade English
courses so that everyone can take up where he or she left off.

MR. HYDE: She's right. We have limited resources and tough decisions
to make. Most of the students are going to college or into farming,
and we have to plan our curriculum with that in mind. How could you
justify setting up a machine shop and hiring another teacher if only
seven or eight students used it?

DORIS: After all, Richard, we can have only one Homecoming queen.

FRED: And one activities editor. Look, Richard, I'm sorry about the
jokes I made, but we have to face facts. We aren't here to reform
Bead-Boot relations. We are supposed to be putting out the best
yearbook we can, and what we have here speaks for itself. You talk
about "fair"--what about Paul? He's worked as hard as Jerry, and
he'll be just as disappointed if he doesn't get the job. I don't
know what his attitude toward Beads is, but surely he isn't responsible for all of their problems. He's entitled to be judged on his
merits . . . on justice.

RICHARD: Justice! Even if I were willing to admit that there is no
official discrimination now, what about the past? Now that we're
up here in our ivory tower, you are ready to say, "Okay, now let's
be fair."

MRS. JENKINS: I can certainly sympathize with your feelings, Richard.
There are a lot of Jefferson graduates who could justifiably feel
resentful about the raw deal they got while they were here. But
what can we do for them? Even if something could be done, as Fred
said, it's not our job.

MR. HYDE: Let's not rule out the possibility of changing our selection
procedure, even though our doing so would certainly cause pressure
to make similar changes in many other school policies. We want to
be fair to both Jerry and Paul, and either of them could come up

with valid complaints if he is turned down. Can any of us say for
sure what effects changing our policy would have on the quality of
the yearbook? We want to improve Boot-Bead relations. Might not a
change make them even worse? This is bound to be an important and
controversial decision. What shall we do?

Questions

1. How would Richard have defined "fair"? How might Fred have
defined "fair"? Would looking up "fair" and "justice" in the dictionary
settle the argument? Explain.

2. Do you think that Fred and Richard might define their terms
differently under other circumstances? Explain.

3. What arguments do you think Paul might make to the committee if
he didn't get the job?

4. Suppose Paul sued the school for giving the position to Jerry.
What arguments do you think his lawyer might make to the court?

5. Answer questions 3 and 4 from the viewpoint of Jerry.

6. Could this problem be resolved by compromise? If so, how? If not, why not?

7. This story is about "Beads" and "Boots." Can you think of any other groups they might resemble, past or present?

8. Do you think a quota system or reverse discrimination can ever be justifiable in our society? Give reasons for your answer.

9. Has your thinking about this issue changed during the course of this lesson? Explain how and why.

LESSON 2: THE PROPOSED EQUAL RIGHTS AMENDMENT

By Ruby Jiminez, Darcy Lobdell, Jane Parks, and Steve Warren

Overview

This lesson contains the following student materials:

Assignment 1. A fictional account about two students who have applied for the job of library assistant in a high school. One is male and the other is female. Both students have strong and weak points, and some of these are related to sexual factors.

Assignment 2. The full text of the proposed Equal Rights Amendment.

Assignment 3. A brief history of the background of the proposed ERA.

Assignment 4. A summary of equal-rights provisions in existing federal laws.

Assignment 5. Sample arguments for and against ratification of the proposed ERA.

Lesson Objectives

Students will be able to *recognize a problem for inquiry* (To what extent should rights be made equal for males and females?) and *offer hypotheses* in response to it after a discussion of Assignment 1. *Testing the validity of the hypotheses* can then occur as the students examine material in Assignments 2, 3, 4, and 5. Finally, after evaluating the arguments presented in Assignment 5, students will be able to *form and support generalizations* about whether women and men should have constitutionally guaranteed equal rights in most, if not all, aspects of American life.

Intended Student Audience: Grades 9-12.

Suggested Time for Classroom Use of Materials: Three to five class periods.

Specific Objectives

Cognitive Objectives. Upon completion of this lesson students will:

knowledge goals

1. Know what is stated in the proposed Equal Rights Amendment.

2. Be familiar with the history of the proposed ERA.

3. Be able to cite representative arguments of those favoring and those opposing ratification of the ERA.

skill development   4. Be able to read, compare, recall, and interpret information about the proposed ERA.

5. Recognize this central problem for inquiry: Should women and men have constitutionally guaranteed equal rights in almost all aspects of American life?

6. Be able to form hypotheses in response to the central problem for inquiry.

7. Be able to test the validity of their hypotheses by examining sample arguments for and against ratification of the proposed ERA.

8. Be able to form and support generalizations about whether women and men should have constitutionally guaranteed equal rights in most if not all aspects of American life.

<u>Affective Objectives</u>. Upon completion of this lesson students will:

empathy   1. Understand and be able to explain the views of those both favoring and opposed to adoption of the ERA.

social participation   2. Be willing to participate in group discussions while examining information about the proposed ERA.

values clarification   3. Be willing to attempt to objectively analyze both their own values and those held by others in regard to the topic of equal rights for women and men.

tolerance   4. Be willing to tolerate (but not necessarily agree with) a variety of conflicting viewpoints on a controversial topic.

Teaching Suggestions

Introducing the Lesson

Begin the lesson by providing each student with a copy of Assignment 1. Ask the class to read it and consider the questions that accompany it. Particular attention should be devoted to questions 4, 5, and 6. Question 4 asks whether sex should be the deciding factor in filling job positions, all other factors being equal. Question 5 relates problems posed by the fictional account in Assignment 1 to the current controversy over ratification of the proposed Equal Rights Amendment. Question 6 requires that the students consider the abstract question of whether women and men should have guaranteed equal rights in most, if not all, aspects of American life--the central problem for inquiry in this lesson.

Record the students' responses to question 6 on the chalkboard, and ask if any of these responses are similar to the central question posed in the lesson. (If none are similar, add the stated problem for inquiry to the list of student responses.) Ask the students to attempt to answer this question, giving reasons for their answers. Do the answers vary? If not, why not? If so, how and why? Students' answers to the topic question at this point probably will be tentative. Point out to the students that these initial answers will be used as hypotheses, and that they will be expected to reconsider and change their first responses as they examine the material in the assignments that follow.

Continuing the Lesson

Assignments 2, 3, and 4 provide information about what the proposed ERA actually states, a brief history of the proposed ERA, and a summary of the equal-rights provisions of existing federal laws. These assignments can be duplicated and given to the students as a package. Discussion ought to focus on the questions that follow each assignment, with particular attention given to students' attitudes toward the proposed ERA: Is it really necessary? What do the terms "equal" and "discrimination" mean? How do their meanings differ? What do the two terms mean in the context of the proposed ERA? After the discussion, you might again remind the students that their opinions about the proposed ERA may change, especially after they examine the sample arguments presented in

Assignment 5.

Assignment 5 could be used with students in a variety of of ways. One method would be to divide the students into two groups and assign each group to study only one side of the arguments. The two groups could then debate the merits of the proposed amendment. A second method would be to ask small groups to consider all the arguments and report on which ones seem the most reasonable or valid. Students should be encouraged to come up with additional arguments both for and against ratification.

During a discussion of the history of the ERA (Assignment 3), you might mention that in February 1978 the Virginia House Privileges and Election Committee again failed to recommend approval of the ERA for that state's full legislature. The vote in the committee against recommendation was 12-8. In March 1978, during the governor's temporary absence from the state of Kentucky, Lt. Gov. Thelma Stovall vetoed an attempt by the Kentucky legislature to rescind its earlier approval of the ERA.

When discussing the pros and cons related to the ERA and military service in Assignment 5, you may want to point out that women ROTC cadets are now scoring very high on advanced physical fitness tests, and that the U.S. Army and Air Force have had women generals since 1971, the Navy since 1972, and the Marine Corps since 1978. Not all military officials are equally accepting of this situation, however. Gen. John K. Singlaub, then chief of staff of the U.S. Armed Forces Command, said in early 1978 that he did not favor assigning women to combat roles. Gen. Robert L. Nichols, deputy chief of staff for manpower for the Marine Corps, and his Navy counterpart, Vice Adm. James D. Watkins, chief of naval personnel, agreed with Singlaub. The Army and the Air Force personnel chiefs, on the other hand, felt that the head of each service should have the option of deciding whether to send females into combat zones.

On the subject of sports and the ERA, you might remind the class that the number of women participating in college varsity sports has risen from about 50,000 in 1974 to more than 100,000 in 1977. According to the Association for Intercollegiate Athletics for Women, females received 200 athletic scholarships in 1971. In 1977 about 350 U.S.

colleges and universities awarded athletic scholarships to women.

Some students might be interested in doing research about how their own state legislature has acted in regard to the proposed ERA and how most people in their city or state feel about granting equal rights to women.

Concluding the Lesson

End the lesson by asking students to consider how they would now respond to Question 4 in Assignment 5. Specifically, they could be asked to complete the following topic sentence, supporting their answers with reasons and examples: "The proposed Equal Rights Amendment (should/should not) become a part of our federal Constitution because. . . ."

Optional Teaching Strategies

If you decide to use this lesson early in the school year, students could further expand and evaluate their responses if it were used in conjunction with an examination of one or more of the following issues in U.S. history:

1. The efforts of individual women through four centuries to assert their rights, among them Anne Hutchinson in the 1600s; Abigail Adams in the 1700s; Margaret Fuller, Lucretia Mott, Elizabeth Cady Stanton, and Susan B. Anthony in the 1800s; Betty Freidan, Kate Millett, Germaine Greer, Billie Jean King, Bella Abzug, Gloria Steinem, and Shirley Chisholm in the 1900s.

2. The Seneca Falls New York Women's Rights Convention of 1848.

3. Debates over passage of the 19th Amendment to the U.S. Constitution.

4. Discrimination practiced toward blacks, Mexican Americans, Indians, and Japanese Americans from the early 1800s to 1964.

Additional Reading

Brown, Barbara A., et al. "The Equal Rights Amendment: A Constitutional Basis for Equal Rights for Women." *Yale Law Review,* April 1971, pp. 872-981.

Cohn, Ellen. "Women Must Make Time for Equal Rights." *Politiks,* March 28, 1978, pp. 17-18.

"Continuing Controversy Over the Women's Equal Rights Amendment." *Congressional Digest,* June/July 1977.

D'Aulaire, Emily and Per Ola. "Equal Rights Amendment: What's It All About?" *Reader's Digest,* February 1977, pp. 98-102.

"Fighting the ERA: The Ladies Mobilize." *Texas Observer,* November 15, 1974, pp. 1, 3-5.

Freund, Paul A. "The Equal Rights Amendment Is Not the Way." *Harvard Civil Rights/Civil Liberties Law Review,* March 1971, pp. 234-242.

Phyllis Schlafly Report (Box 618, Alton, Illinois 62002), all issues.

"Pro and Con—Should Women Fight in War?" *U.S. News and World Report,* February 13, 1978, pp. 53-54.

"Should There Be National Service for Women?" Gallup Youth Survey, August 3, 1977.

Streshinsky, Shirley. "Points to Ponder: Shirley Streshinsky on the Not-So-Weaker Sex." *Reader's Digest,* November 1976, pp. 83, 85.

Teaching American History: The Quest for Relevancy. 44th Yearbook of the National Council for the Social Studies, 1974. (Contains an extensive bibliography of women in American society.)

Whelan, Elizabeth M. "Myth of the Liberated Housewife" and "Should a Career Woman Have Children?" *Harper's,* February 1977, pp. 101, 153, 157-58, 165.

Will, George F. "Stacking the Deck on ERA." *Newsweek,* November 14, 1977, p. 128.

STUDENT MATERIALS FOR LESSON 2

Lesson 2, Assignment 1

WHO SHOULD GET THE JOB?

Imagine the situation described below and answer the questions
that follow.

Janet is a new student at Greenwood High School. She has applied
for the job of library assistant. John has also applied for the job.
Only one assistant is hired every semester.

Janet worked as a library assistant at her previous school. She
was, specifically, a book filer, a job which entails the lifting of
heavy books. She might have found this very strenuous work, but there
were always people around to help her. Janet wants the job so she can
learn more about library science, the field in which she plans to major
in college. Janet understands the call-number system, but she can't be
expected to lift as many books as a male candidate for the job.

John has never worked in a library. However, he is bright, and he
is easily capable of lifting a stack of heavy books. John wants the job
so he can earn money for future college expenses. Although he might be
slow at filing until he learns the call-number system, he would be able
to lift many books at a time.

You, the principal, must make the choice. Would you choose Janet
or John?

Questions

1. In this imaginary situation, who is Janet? Who is John?

2. What are some problems that might arise if you hired John?
If you hired Janet?

3. What should be the determining factors in your decision about which applicant to hire?

4. Do you think a person's sex should be the deciding factor for a job, all other factors being equal? Explain your answer.

5. Can you think of any current controversial issue that has any similarities to this story?

6. Suppose you had to give this lesson a new title, also in the form of a question. What would be the question? (In your question, do *not* include the words "Janet," "John," "library," or "principal.")

Lesson 2, Assignment 2

THE TEXT OF THE PROPOSED ERA

What follows is the text of the proposed Equal Rights Amendment, or ERA. If ratified by the legislatures of three-fourths (38) of the states, it will become the 27th amendment to the U.S. Constitution. Read all three sections and answer the questions below.

Section I: Equality of rights under the law shall not be denied or abridged by the United States or by any state on account of sex.

Section II: The Congress shall have the power to enforce, by appropriate legislation, the provisions of this article.

Section III: This amendment shall take effect two years after ratification.

Questions

1. Do you think the term "equality of rights" should be interpreted to mean the rights of both men and women in *all* situations?

2. What situations and issues might be affected by passage of the first section of the proposed ERA?

3. Do you think this amendment could take away the rights of states to legislate in this area? Explain.

4.   At this point, what is your opinion of the ERA? Why do you hold this opinion?

Lesson 2, Assignment 3

A BRIEF HISTORY OF THE ERA

Here is a brief history of the ERA. Read it and answer the questions that follow.

The proposed ERA has a rich history. It began in North America in 1648, when Margaret Brent asked the House of Delegates in the colony of Maryland to allow women to vote and hold public office there. The proposal was refused, as were similar later requests to male representatives by such women as Abigail Adams, Elizabeth Cady Stanton, Susan B. Anthony, and Alice Paul. However, women finally did receive federal enfranchisement with passage of the 19th Amendment in 1920. Twelve states had already granted women the right to vote.

The next major move by advocates of women's rights came in 1923 when a proposal similar to the current ERA was introduced for consideration by Congress. Yet little came of this proposal until it was reintroduced in 1969. From that point events moved quickly, with the help of Representative Martha Griffiths. On March 22, 1972, Congress approved the measure and submitted it to the states for ratification or rejection.

Many states ratified rapidly, but opposition soon appeared, and the campaign for approval of the ERA first slowed and then stalled.

The ERA must be approved by 38 states in order for the proposal to become a part of our federal Constitution. The deadline at writing was March 22, 1979. By June 1978 35 states had approved the amendment--three short of the required number. Three states had rescinded their ratification, though the legality of this action was being challenged. The desirability of instituting a three- to seven-year extension of the ratification deadline was being debated throughout 1977 and 1978.

Questions

1. Name some women throughout our history who have worked for expanded rights for members of their sex.

81

2.   When was an earlier version of the ERA first introduced in Congress?

3.   When was the present ERA approved by both houses of Congress?

4.   How many state legislatures must approve the ERA for ratification? How many had approved it by June 1978?

EQUAL RIGHTS PROVISIONS IN EXISTING LAWS

Many state laws forbid discrimination on the basis of sex in such areas as pay scales, access to land, conditions of employment, use of state funds, and access to consumer credit. However, existing laws are not the same in all 50 states, nor do they cover all areas of possible sex discrimination.

There are also many existing federal laws prohibiting sex discrimination. After reading the brief summaries of these laws that follow, answer the questions at the end of this assignment.

Fair Labor Standards Act of 1938 (amended in 1963 and 1974). Prohibits discrimination because of sex with respect to the payment of wages for work that requires equal skill, effort, or responsibility and which is performed under equal working conditions. Wage differences between men and women may exist when those differences are based on a seniority system, a merit system, or job-related factors.

Civil Rights Act of 1964. Prohibits employment discrimination on the basis of sex unless sex is a legitimate occupational qualification. Applies to any employer of 15 or more persons in work that results in interstate commerce.

Nurse Training Act of 1971. Forbids discrimination on the basis of sex in regard to admission to any federally assisted school that trains people for health professions.

Comprehensive Health Manpower Act of 1971. Prohibits the use of federal funds in programs which discriminate on the basis of sex in schools of medicine, osteopathy, dentistry, veterinary medicine, optometry, pharmacy, podiatry, public health, and nursing.

Higher Education Act of 1972. Extends a 1963 amendment to the Fair Labor Standards Act to include the executive, administrative, and professional employees of educational institutions. Forbids sex discrimination in all federally assisted programs. Mandates equal funding for male and female athletic programs (by Title IX).

Equal Employment Opportunity Act of 1972. Set up a commission which can file suits against employers if their efforts at cooperation do not succeed in eliminating employment discrimination. Covers employees of governments, educational institutions, and businesses or labor unions that employ 15 or more people.

Civil Rights Commission Act of 1972. Allows the Civil Rights Commission to further investigate alleged acts of sex discrimination in all areas involving civil rights.

Comprehensive Employment and Training Act of 1973. Forbids discrimination on the basis of sex, race, creed, color, national origin, political beliefs or affiliation, or philosophical beliefs in programs that receive its benefits.

Federal Equal Credit Opportunity Act of 1975. Forbids discrimination on the basis of sex or marital status in granting credit to consumers.

Questions

1. What general areas or topics are covered in these equal rights provisions of federal law? (One area, for example, would be "payment of wages.")

2. Do all states have the same equal rights laws?

3. Do you think these laws are sufficient to ensure equal rights for *both* men and women? Explain your answer.

The material is this lesson is based on "The Continuing Controversy Over the Women's Equal Rights Amendment," *Congressional Digest,* June/ July 1977, p. 166.

Lesson 2, Assignment 5

ARGUMENTS FOR AND AGAINST THE ERA

In recent years the proposed ERA has generated many heated debates. Some examples of the arguments used in both support of and opposition to ERA ratification are presented in this assignment. As you examine them, consider (1) which ones seem the most reasonable or valid to you and (2) what other arguments both for and against the proposed ERA you can think of. Then answer the questions at the end of the assignment.

The Military

Arguments for the ERA

The U.S. Constitution gives Congress the power to "raise and support armies" and to "provide and maintain a navy." It is up to Congress to decide how many people, if any, will be required to serve and how they will be selected.

A young man can now enlist in our military service without a high school degree; a young woman must have such a degree.

Those women who are physically or mentally unqualified for the draft, or who are conscientious objectors, or who are exempt because of their responsibilities (such as certain public officials or women with dependents) will not have to serve, just as men who are

Arguments against the ERA

If adopted, the ERA would allow no military exemptions on the basis of sex.

Morale in the U.S. Armed Forces would suffer with passage of the ERA.

A Roper Poll of 1971 showed that 77 percent of American women do not want to be subject to the draft.

Congress already has the power to make West Point, the U.S. Army, and all combat units totally female if it wants to do so; indeed, Congress has always had full authority over these matters. Enacting a Constitutional amendment to force Congress to change these laws is an extravagant substitute for a mere majority in the House and

unqualified or exempt would not serve. Congress could also decide to exempt from the draft all parents of children under 18.

Many other countries have integrated women into military combat units without experiencing problems.

Women are physically and mentally better conditioned than men and have a longer life expectancy.

In ROTC programs, many women have achieved perfect scores on their physical fitness tests.

Women are physically capable of doing many duties required of men in the military service.

In 1978 the Pentagon asked to be able to assign women to combat zones and duty. Many military officers now believe that women can handle this.

Most patriotic American girls would want to fight to protect their country. Many have served in other capacities in combat zones since the days of the American Revolution, and nurses have served at the front lines during all of our wars.

Senate.

Compulsory military conscription (the draft) and combat duty would be the same for both sexes if the ERA were ratified.

It is never easy to bid sons goodbye as they leave for service, but it is easier to accept a son's role in the defense of his country than to see a daughter go. Emotionally, most mothers prepare for their sons' possible service all the years they are growing. It is not a situation which women can accept for their daughters.

Family Life

Arguments for the ERA

Homosexuals are being deprived of rights because of their sexual preference. The ERA will help end discrimination on the basis of sexual preference.

Working mothers are now being discriminated against. Just because they work does not mean that they neglect their children. It is not true that the total responsibility for child care lies with the mother.

The ERA would not force any wife to go out and work for a living.

Just as giving women the right to vote in 1920 did not lead to the breakup of families, nor would passage of the ERA.

In states that have already passed ERAs, no one has interpreted the law as allowing husbands to leave their wives without support, nor have homosexual marriages been sanctioned (unless they had previously been legitimized prior to passage of the law).

State laws calling for a husband to support his wife specify no more than the duty to provide "necessaries." State laws usually

Arguments against the ERA

Under the ERA, denying a marriage license to two homosexuals would not be permissible. Thus homosexuals would be allowed to marry and to have the same rights, tax benefits, and social acceptance as normal married couples. Married homosexuals would also be allowed to *adopt children*.

The ERA would threaten the institution of the family--a basic concept to the Judeo-Christian ethic and to the values of a free society. Under the ERA, choosing motherhood or homemaking as a primary job could be disadvantageous for all women.

The task of providing nurture to children ordinarily falls to the housewife and mother. Intelligent societies have imposed upon husbands and fathers the primary responsibility for supporting their wives and children. Traditionally, laws have decreed that a woman who has devoted her life to housekeeping and motherhood shall receive some provision from the estate of her husband when she becomes his widow.

allow the husband, not the wife, to decide what constitutes "necessaries."

As it stands now, all marital property legally belongs to the husband. A widow can retain only 50 percent of the family property after her husband's death. The ERA strives not only for a moral partnership but also for an economically equal partnership.

Many men are in favor of the ERA because they are often discriminated against in such areas as family support. In many states, divorced men are required to pay alimony even if the wife makes a substantial salary or remarries.

In essence, the amendment would simply require *equality*. Alimony could be granted to men as well as women, and both the mother and father would be held legally responsible for the support of their children. Furthermore, ERA would not deprive women of any *enforceable* rights of support. Courts do not interfere with ongoing marriages, and child support isn't collectible in most cases.

The ERA would wipe out the financial obligation of a husband to his wife and children, thus mandating a completely new principle of support.

Women would gain new responsibilities for family support, while similar obligations for men would be reduced.

In essence, this amendment would make great changes in laws pertaining to the family. Women would lose their right *not* to work and their claims to alimony and child support. (As for child support, it is *collectible*. In the Houston, Texas, area, for example, 50 percent of all fathers ordered to pay child support do so.) Present laws are not perfect, but why remove their protection from families? Under the ERA, a mother could be held equally responsible for the support of children, and thus be forced to leave her home and go to work.

Education and Sports

Arguments for the ERA

The ERA would provide a constitutional basis for equality of funding in scholastic sports programs, which is now guaranteed only by an act of Congress that could be changed by new legislation or a court ruling.

Women can participate in and have always participated in many of the same sports that men enjoy. Since 1934, women's athletic records have been rising fast. Participation in athletics by both sexes should be encouraged because it promotes fitness.

The ERA would not require educational and athletic quotas for men and women, nor would it require that student bodies accurately reflect the sex distribution in the population. Rather, the amendment would require that educational admission be granted on the basis of ability and that scholarship funds be fairly distributed to students of both sexes.

Arguments against the ERA

If the ERA is adopted, private schools and colleges that now admit only girls or only boys would be required to become fully coeducational.

The ERA would deprive students of the freedom of choice to attend an all-girls' or all-boys' school. All sports, including contact sports, would have to be coeducational for both practice and competition. This policy is bad because girls cannot compete on an equal basis with boys. Besides, equal funding for women's and men's scholastic athletic programs is now guaranteed by law.

Employment and Benefits

Arguments for the ERA

Women are discriminated against in the job market. Furthermore, several states have so-called protective laws which restrict the occupations or conditions of employment of females and limit the number of hours women may work. These restrictions may prevent women from being promoted.

Many women must work to help support their families. More women than ever are heads of households, and in many cases they are the sole support of their children.

Woman are not taking away men's jobs. They make up only 40 percent of the nation's working force.

Many men favor adoption of the ERA because it will make the social security system more equitable. They argue that since the average male life span is shorter than that of women, they should be able to retire and receive social security earlier than age 65.

Arguments against the ERA

The ERA, if adopted, will wipe out protective labor laws, forcing women employed in factory and service occupations to do "men's work."

Our social security system presently *favors* women. For example, women can begin drawing payments if they retire at 62, while men must wait until they reach 65.

Sex Roles and Identity

Arguments for the ERA

Granting women the right to vote in 1920 did not cause women to become men or more masculine.

A Harris Poll in 1976 showed that more than 62 percent of U.S. residents favored adoption of the proposed ERA.

The ERA simply allows women the legally guaranteed right to be able to choose or compete for on an equal basis whatever roles they wish to assume or pursue.

No one sex, nationality, or race of people has a monopoly on the desire for human fulfillment. The ERA does not seek to make men and women the same; rather, it seeks to ensure that the two sexes have equal rights and responsibilities.

Arguments against the ERA

The ERA is unrealistic in its implication that men and women are identical legal beings with exactly the same rights and responsibilities at all times and under all circumstances. In its attempt to enforce this assumption, the amendment resembles Procrustes, the fabled robber of ancient Greece who stretched or mutilated his victims to make them conform to the length of his bed.

God gave men the capacity to beget children and women the capacity to bear them. A newborn child is the most helpless of creatures, and children require many years of nurture and training before they can grow into intelligent beings capable of functioning as adults. The ERA devalues this role, which God meant to be performed by mothers. God made man and woman to be different—equal partners in life, but not the same. Thus the law must treat men and women separately and not subject them to the same rules.

Privacy

Arguments for the ERA

It is not true that the ERA would prohibit separate sleeping, bathing, and toilet facilities in public institutions, colleges, prisons, and military barracks.

No legislation can "go beyond the bedroom door" to regulate personal behavior or mandate which spouse makes the major home decisions.

No state which already has a law similar to the ERA has established coed restrooms or other such facilities.

Arguments against the ERA

If adopted, the ERA could make all public restroom facilities available to both sexes. This would be a violation of individual privacy.

The ERA could give the federal government the power to decide which spouse can rule the home and make major decisions for the family.

State Laws and State Sovereignty

Arguments for the ERA

The ERA would not change state laws except to make them apply equally to women. For example, if a state law says that a father may sue for damages if his child is injured but denies the same privilege to a mother (as is the case in Utah), the law would have to be changed to say that both parents may sue for damages. If a law says that boy scouts may fly a flag over the state capitol building but girl scouts may not (as is the case in Oklahoma), the law would have to be changed to allow all scouts to fly a flag over the capitol. If a law says that money from room rentals in a home belongs to the husband (as is the case in North Carolina), the law would have to be changed to say that the money belongs to both spouses. If the law says that a 10-year-old boy may have a newspaper route but that a 17-year-old girl cannot (as is the case in Alabama), the law would have to be changed so that the same age limits apply to both sexes.

Although state or federal laws

Arguments against the ERA

Individual states have passed many laws to buttress the federal laws, orders, and regulations outlawing discrimination on the basis of sex. We have too many laws already. The ERA would only add another law that would take away some of our freedom to decide how people should be treated.

Probably the greatest danger posed by the ERA lies in Section 2, which provides that Congress will have the power of enforcement. This means that the executive branch will administer the ERA and the federal courts will adjucate it. Section 2 would give the federal government control over the last remaining aspects of our life that have not been federally regulated, among them marriage, divorce, and child custody.

The ERA would transfer from the states to the federal government powers which have been reserved for the states throughout our country's history. By doing so, the amendment will be in conflict with the intent of

have eliminated much sex discrimination, a law passed by one legislature can be revoked by a sub-
sequent session. The ERA would
make equal rights a constitutional
and permanent reality.

If the federal government had
not intervened, many states probably would still have laws that
discriminate against minority
groups. Moreover, if the 19th
Amendment had not been passed,
it is doubtful whether many
states would have given women
the right to vote. The same
can be said for the 26th
Amendment, which grants 18-
year-olds the right to vote.

We have too many state and
federal laws today that deal
with sex discrimination. Many
could be abolished if the ERA
were adopted.

the Constitution to create "an
indestructible union composed
of indestructible states" and
will reduce the states in large
measure to powerless nonentities.

Traditionally, it has been
left to the states to regulate
such matters as marriage, the
care and custody of children,
divorce, and other social institutions. Each state has been
able to make laws that are con-
gruent with the moral beliefs
and convictions of most of its
residents. The ERA would
abolish this prerogative.

Legal Status

Arguments for the ERA

Our federal Constitution was framed according to the concepts of English Common Law, which does not regard women as "legal persons." The ERA would eliminate that deficiency by determining ownership of property on the basis of the value of each spouse's contribution to its acquisition. This provision would afford real dignity to the roles of housewife and mother. A woman would at long last be considered a "person" under the law.

The only right constitutionally guaranteed to women is the right to vote. Other constitutional rights accruing to women have been awarded only through case-by-case rulings or law-by-law decisions.

The courts have upheld sex distinctions in the law despite the due-process clause in the Fifth Amendment and the equal-protection clause in the Fourteenth Amendment. In Section 2 of the Fourteenth Amendment the word "male" appears three times; thus discrimination on the basis of sex was actually written into

Arguments against the ERA

Since 1971 the U.S. Supreme Court has issued at least eight rulings implying that ratification of the ERA is not necessary to remove any legal discriminations to which women may be subjected. In all these cases, the court held that any law—federal or state—which makes distinctions between the legal rights and responsibilities of men and those of women is unconstitutional unless the distinction is based upon reasonable grounds and is designed to protect women in some specific situation.

Acts of Congress, executive orders of the president, and many federal regulations prohibit discrimination on the basis of sex in education, employment, financing, housing, public accommodations, and all other federal activities. Moreover, these same acts, orders, and regulations forbid states and their subdivisions and all private persons to discriminate on the basis of sex in any activity of any nature which is financed in whole or in part by

our Constitution. Just as freedom from discrimination based on race, color, or creed is a part of our Constitution, so should freedom from discrimination on the basis of sex. Because women are not presently considered "persons" under the Constitution, we need the ERA to give them their full legal rights.

federal funds. Since so many activities in America are supported by federal funds, these acts, orders, and regulations protect women from discrimination in virtually all areas of American life.

Present constitutional guarantees--especially the equal-protection-of-the-law clause in the Fourteenth Amendment--provide amply for the initiation of enabling legislation and law enforcement to overcome the deprivation of rights; the same steps would be necessary even if the ERA were ratified. Legislation can address specific lems in a way that no constitutional provision can.

The ERA is simply unnecessary. Women are already covered by the Fifth and Fourteenth Amendments. The Fourteenth Amendment already guarantees "equal protection of the laws" to every "person." The word "person" obviously must be interpreted to apply to every woman as well as to every member of a racial minority.

The Fifth Amendment says that "no person" shall be deprived of life, liberty, or property with-

out due process of law. In
more than 180 cases, federal
courts have ruled that women
are "persons" under the Fourteenth Amendment.

Questions

1.   In which category did you find the *least* reasonable or valid
arguments for or against passage of the ERA? Why?

   a.   The Military   e.   Employment and Benefits

   b.   Family Life   f.   State Laws and Sovereignty

   c.   Education and Sports   g.   Privacy

   d.   Sex Roles and Identity   h.   Legal Status

2.   In which category did you find the *most* reasonable arguments?
Why?

3.   What other arguments might you add to those provided in the
lesson materials?

4.   Imagine that you were asked to vote for or against passage of the proposed ERA. How would you vote, and why?

The sample arguments in this lesson are based on "The Continuing Controversy Over Women's Rights Amendment," *Congressional Digest,* June/ July 1977, pp. 170-191.

LESSON 3: THE DAVID MARSTON CASE

By Alicia Bell, Rachel De Leon, Nat Sawyer, and John Stevenson

Overview

This lesson contains the following student materials:

Assignment 1. A fictional account about the effects of patronage on a high school athletic department.

Assignment 2. A brief history of political patronage and the spoils system in American politics.

Assignment 3. A summary of the David Marston issue and sample arguments for and against his dismissal as a U.S. attorney by President Jimmy Carter in 1977.

Lesson Objectives

Students will be able to *recognize a problem for inquiry* (When is a patronage system justifiable?) and *offer hypotheses* in response to it after a discussion of Assignment 1. *Testing the validity of the hypotheses* can then occur as the students examine material in Assignments 2 and 3. Finally, after evaluating the arguments presented in Assignment 3, students will be able to *form and support generalizations* about whether political patronage is good or bad.

Intended Student Audience: Grades 9-12.

Suggested Time for Classroom Use of Materials: One to two class periods.

Specific Objectives

Cognitive Objectives. Upon completion of this lesson the students will:

knowledge goals	1.	Be able to define "political patronage," "merit system," and "spoils system."
	2.	Be familiar with the history of political patronage as it developed in our political process.
	3.	Know how data about the David Marston case can be used to raise many questions about the good and bad aspects of political patronage as it is exercised with the American political process.
skill development	4.	Be able to compare, recall, and interpret information about the application of political patronage in United States history.

5. Recognize this central problem for inquiry: Should political appointments be based mainly on merit or on party patronage?

6. Be able to form hypotheses in response to the central problem for inquiry.

7. Be able to test the validity of the hypotheses by examining sample arguments for and against the uses of political patronage.

8. Be able to form and support generalizations about the worth of political patronage.

Affective Objectives. Upon completion of this lesson students will:

empathy
1. Understand and be able to explain the views of both those who favor and those who are opposed to political patronage.

social participation
2. Be willing to participate in group discussions to examine information about the uses of political patronage.

values clarification
3. Be willing to attempt to analyze objectively both their own values and those held by others in regard to the application of political patronage.

tolerance
4. Be willing to tolerate (but not necessarily agree with) a variety of conflicting viewpoints on a controversial topic.

Teaching Suggestions

Introducing the Lesson

Begin the lesson by providing each student with a copy of Assignment 1. Ask the class to read it and consider the accompanying questions. Particular attention should be devoted to questions 2 and 4. Question 2 asks students to hypothesize about the uses and worth of a patronage system, with its inherent rewards for previous favors, as opposed to a merit system as the basis for deciding employment. Question 4 requires students to consider the following abstract question on the basis of their responses to question 2: Should job appointments be based mainly on the basis of merit or on a system of patronage? Since this is the central question for inquiry in this lesson, record sample student responses on the chalkboard and ask for reasons to support the answers. Remind the students that they will have the opportunity to change their responses and reasons after examining Assignments 2 and 3.

Continuing the Lesson

Assignment 2 contains a brief history of political patronage and the spoils system in American politics. After the students have read this assignment, considerable discussion should be devoted to the differences between a government appointment based on political patronage and one based on merit. After the two types of appointments have been discussed, and examples given of each, ask students to list some of the virtues and drawbacks of both kinds of appointments. This discussion can serve to introduce Assignment 3, which consists of a summary of the David Marston issue and sample arguments for and against his dismissal by President Carter.

Before students begin to examine the material in Assignment 3, refer them to the campaign statement made by President Carter about merit appointments of governmental officials (last paragraph of Assignment 2). Point out that federal judges and federal prosecutors (called "U.S. attorneys") are not covered by the civil service merit system for governmental appointments. While they usually possess excellent qualifications, non-civil-service employees of the federal government are nevertheless chosen through a system of political patronage. Generally, but not always, a president appoints members of his own party to such federal positions. (One exception was the 1978 appointment by President Carter, a Democrat, of William H. Webster, a Republican and a federal judge from Missouri, to head the Federal Bureau of Investigation.)

Assignment 3 can be examined in two stages. The first stage might focus on reading and discussion of the background of the Marston issue. Students can then be divided into groups and asked to discuss which of the arguments supporting and opposing Marston's firing seem the most reasonable or to have the greatest merit and which seem the least reasonable and to have the least merit.

Consideration of the questions that follow the pros and cons about the Marston issue can help students assess the worth of each argument and add other arguments of their own.

In facilitating the discussion, you might point out that just prior to Marston's firing the FBI's Philadelphia bureau had rated him an "excellent" federal prosecutor, though some people believed that he was politicizing his federal office. You may also want to remind the students that at the time of Marston's firing, Representative Flood was being investigated by both the U.S. Attorney's Office in Philadelphia and the U.S. House Ethics Committee for alleged bribery connections. (Stephen Elko, a former Flood aide, had alleged that about $100,000 had been paid to Flood to persuade him to use his political influence to arrange funding for a new hospital.) These other points might also be offered for student consideration:

1. On January 12, 1978, Attorney General Griffin Bell stated that he had intended to replace Marston much earlier but postponed doing so because he felt such an action might disrupt some investigations in progress.

Marston himself was a political appointee, having obtained his job just four months before Carter became president. Marston got the job through the efforts of his former boss, Senator Richard Schweiker, and former Senator Hugh Scott, both Republicans from Pennsylvania.

3. In 1977 President Carter signed an executive order that established commissions in the 11 U.S. Appeals Court circuits for the purpose of recommending federal judges for panels. A Justice Department spokes-

person said that Carter decided not to establish such commissions to recommend U.S. District Court judges and U.S. attorneys because of opposition in the Senate.

Concluding the Lesson

The lesson can be concluded with a discussion of question 4 in Assignment 3 and the summary questions that follow. All but the last of the summary questions require students to review arguments for and against the use of political patronage. Students can use the last summary question as the basis for forming and supporting generalizations about basing political appointments on patronage as opposed to merit. Ask them to complete the following topic sentence and support their responses with reasons and examples: "Political appointments should (always/sometimes/never) be based on patronage."

Optional Teaching Strategies

If you use this lesson early in the school year, students could further expand and evaluate their responses in conjunction with an examination of one or more of the following topics in U.S. history:

1. The case of *Marbury vs. Madison* in 1803.

2. The emergence of the spoils system on a large scale during the presidency of Andrew Jackson.

3. The reasons for passage of the Pendleton Act of 1883.

4. The problems associated with political patronage and the general growth of our two-party system in the 19th century.

5. Bossism as it was practiced in large cities in the United States from the late 19th century to the mid-20th century.

Additional Reading

"Decision That Backfired on Carter." *U.S. News and World Report,* January 23, 1978, p. 65.

Dye, Thomas R., and L. Harmon Zeigler. *The Irony of Democracy: An Uncommon Introduction to American Politics,* 3rd ed. Belmont, Calif.: Duxbury Press, 1975.

Holt, Don, and Diane Camper. "Justice: The Marston Affair." *Newsweek,* January 30, 1978, p. 34.

LeMann, Nicholas. "The Case for Political Patronage." *Washington Monthly,* December 1977, pp. 8-17.

Post, C. Gordon, Frances P. DeLancy, and Fredryc R. Darby. *Basic Constitutional Cases.* Fairlawn, N.J.: Oxford University Press, 1948.

Roeder, Bill. "Bell Takes the Rap." *Newsweek,* February 6, 1978, p. 13.

Saar, John. "The Philadelphia Story." *New Times,* February 20, 1978, pp. 25-33.

Shrum, Robert. "On the Hiring and Firing of U.S. Attorneys." *New Times,* February 20, 1978, p. 34.

"Tangled Scandal, A." *Newsweek,* February 27, 1978, p. 24.

STUDENT MATERIALS FOR LESSON 3

Lesson 3, Assignment 1

TROUBLE IN THE LOCKER ROOM

Imagine the following situation and then answer the questions at the end of the assignment.

You attend one of the largest high schools in an urban area. Maintaining a successful athletic program has always been very important to the students, school administrators, and the community. In recent months the program has deteriorated, and consequently the athletic director has been fired--an action that stirred up considerable hostility.

The school district soon hires a new athletic director, mainly on the basis of recommendations from several coaches at other schools in the district. Everything seems to be getting back to normal, and expectations for another good athletic season are high. Then, without warning and only two weeks after being hired, the new athletic director fires your school's head coach and his top three assistants. Once again the school is in turmoil. Besides being popular with the students and community, all are considered knowledgeable, competent, and hard-working classroom teachers. The new athletic director replaces these coaches with four new people who he claims are equally competent and whom he feels he can work with more comfortably. These four new coaches are the same people who helped the new athletic director get his job.

Questions

1. In this imaginary situation, what did the new athletic director do that provoked controversy?

2. If you were a student at this school, would you have supported the actions of the new athletic director? Explain why or why not.

3. Would you change your attitude if in six months your football team had advanced to the state playoffs? Explain your answer.

4. What sort of general question is raised in this lesson? (When you formulate your question, do *not* use the words "athletic director," "coach," or "teacher.")

Lesson 3, Assignment 2

POLITICAL PATRONAGE AND THE SPOILS SYSTEM

After reading this explanation of political patronage and the spoils system, answer the questions that follow.

Political patronage is a system whereby the victor in an election rewards some of his or her supporters with appointments to positions in government. This kind of patronage is not new in American government. It goes back to the days when George Washington was president. Washington appointed many qualified people to high positions in government, among them Thomas Jefferson as secretary of state and Alexander Hamilton as secretary of the treasury. Both men had helped Washington and had been influential in the fight for independence.

The system of political patronage grew stronger after the election in 1800 of Thomas Jefferson to the presidency. Jefferson's election symbolized the turnover of political power from the Federalists to the Jeffersonian Republicans. John Adams, a Federalist and the outgoing president, had made scores of appointments to Federalist party members; Jefferson replaced many of these Federalist appointees. Later, in 1829, President Andrew Jackson made even more use of the patronage system to appoint his friends and loyal supporters to office.

The practice of appointing one's personal friends to federal positions, before it was inhibited by the advent of civil service reform in the 1880s, became known as the "spoils system." (The name was derived from an observation attributed to William L. Marcy: "To the victor go the spoils.") Long after civil service reform, which drastically reduced the number of political appointments a president could make, the patronage system continues. When a new administration is installed, whether it is Democratic or Republican, most appointed officials either resign or are fired, to be replaced by members of the victorious political party.

A president still has the power to appoint cabinet members, ambassadors, U.S. Supreme Court justices, other federal judges, and U.S. attorneys. Political party loyalty figures very strongly in these appointments. Except for those that carry life terms, most such offices are filled with

new people every time the administration changes, if the new president
represents a different party then the outgoing chief executive. The
power to make such appointments is granted to the president in Article II,
Section 2 of our federal Constitution:

> . . . and the President shall nominate, and by and with
>
> the advice of the Senate, shall appoint Ambassadors,
>
> other public Ministers and Consuls, Judges of the Supreme
>
> Court, and all other officers of the United States, whose
>
> appointments are not herein provided for, and which shall
>
> be established by law. . . .

Senators from the states in which regional offices are located have
tremendous influence in such presidential appointments, especially if
they are members of the president's party. Since the president cannot
possibly become personally acquainted with every candidate, a senatorial
recommendation means a great deal. Because the senator is directly
responsible to the voters, a check-and-balance system for recommendations
is provided.

Political patronage also exists below the level of the presidency.
Almost all elected officials--mayors, governors, representatives, and
senators--are able to fill several offices with personal appointees.
Naturally, these offices are usually given to strong supporters of the
candidates.

President Jimmy Carter, during his election campaign in 1976, issued
a position paper in which he stated that "all federal judges and prosecutors should be appointed strictly on the basis of merit without any
consideration of political aspects or influence." The term *merit* refers
here to qualifications for the job.

Questions

1. What is the main difference between a political patronage
appointment and a merit appointment?

2. How has the spoils system been a part of our political heritage?
Cite at least three examples.

3. What did President Carter say about the appointment of federal
judges and prosecutors during his election campaign in 1976?

4. Do you see any relationship between the information presented in
this assignment and the material in Assignment 1? Explain.

ARGUMENTS FOR AND AGAINST MARSTON

Read the following background material about the David Marston issue. Then read the sample arguments for and against President Carter's action. Finally, answer the questions at the end of the assignment.

In July 1976 President Gerald Ford, a Republican, appointed a fellow Republican, David Marston, to be U.S. attorney for the eastern part of Pennsylvania. Marston's jurisdiction centered around the city of Philadelphia and its image of political corruption. He was to serve in his new job until 1980. Marston entered the job with little trial experience, but soon he began to attempt to clean up the existing political machine in Philadelphia. Many people believed that he was succeeding. With top-notch trial lawyers as assistants, he brought several prominent Democrats to trial and gained convictions.

With the election of Jimmy Carter as president, Marston realized that the chances of keeping his job were minimal. Nevertheless, he challenged Carter, a Democrat, to keep his campaign promise to select and retain federal judges and attorneys on the basis of merit.

In his search for criminal activities, Marston found some irregularities in a federally funded hospital project. His discovery led to an investigation of the alleged involvement of two members of the U.S. House of Representatives, Democrats Joshua Eilberg and Daniel Flood.

On November 4, 1977, Eilberg placed a call to President Carter asking him to remove Marston from his position. Carter relayed the message to Attorney General Bell, and Marston was relieved of his duties. This action was opposed by many people, mostly Republicans.

In 1978, after completing a probe of the case, the Department of Justice declared that Marston's removal did not constitute obstruction of justice. Meanwhile, Marston had become a candidate for the Republican nomination for governor of Pennsylvania.

The questions raised by Marston's firing were not easily resolved. Arguments both supporting and opposing his removal were nationally publicized. Samples of those arguments follow. As you read them, ask yourself which ones seem to be the most reasonable and to have the greatest merit.

Arguments for Marston's removal	Arguments against Marston's removal
Out of 94 federal prosecutors serving in 1978, 25 were Republicans who had been retained in office. Besides, no president has ever fulfilled every campaign pledge he made before his election to office.	President Carter violated a campaign pledge that he would keep politics out of judicial appointments by appointing all federal prosecutors on the basis of merit, not patronage.
President Carter did not know that David Marston was investigating Joshua Eilberg and Daniel Flood when Attorney General Bell fired Marston. Obviously, the president does not have time to personally check on every recommendation sent to him.	President Carter should have made it a point to know that Joshua Eilberg and Daniel Flood were under investigation by Marston's office before he took responsibility for Marston's removal.
According to Attorney General Bell and House Speaker Thomas (Tip) O'Neill, David Marston should have been fired because he had "politicized" his office.	David Marston was only doing his job when he convicted prominent Democratic leaders. He had convicted some Republican leaders as well.
Attorney General Bell publicly declared that he had decided the previous spring to eventually replace David Marston because he did not have sufficient trial experience.	David Marston was not fired until Carter had been in office for a year. By then Marston had begun investigating Eilberg's and Flood's involvement in the financing of a Philadelphia hospital. Both of these men are Democrats.

The Department of Justice decided that Carter and Bell were not guilty of obstructing justice by firing David Marston.

Because elected officials will be held responsible by the voters for the efficiency of the people they nominate for federal office, they will suggest competent nominees.

Traditionally, many presidential appointments have been made on the basis of recommendations by fellow party members in Congress. To oppose such recommendations could alienate those congressmen and thus stall or defeat proposed legislation.

Too many appointments by merit could sap the strength of the two-party system in America. The strength of a political party is derived in part from being able to reward its followers. (To the victor go the spoils of victory.)

Some sources say that Griffin Bell was so concerned about the issue that he considered resigning from his job as head of the Department of Justice.

Because of the prominence and power of political party machines in American cities, elected officials do not always nominate the most qualified individuals to federal appointive offices.

A president should place merit above congressional good will if the two come into conflict, regardless of the legislative or political outcome.

Political appointments must be made on the basis of merit in order to provide for competent government.

Questions

1. Can you think of any other arguments to add to those presented here?

2. Of the arguments presented, which ones do you think are the most reasonable? Why? Which ones seem to have the least merit?

3. Do you feel that investigation of the Marston issue should be continued? Explain your answer.

4. On the basis of the evidence you now have about the Marston case, what would your position be if you were President Carter? If you were David Marston?

Summary Questions

1. Did your personal political opinions affect your evaluation of this case? Explain.

2. "All governmental positions, elected or appointed, should be based on patronage because American elections are run on a political party system. The party must choose the candidate according to party loyalty as well as his or her qualifications." Do you agree with this statement? Why?

3. Do you feel that political appointments should be based mainly on merit or on patronage? Should the same system be used for all non-governmental jobs?

LESSON 4: RECENT ACTIVITIES OF THE AMERICAN NAZI PARTY

By Walter Levy, Manuel Newburger, Todd Pearson, and Mark Walsh

Overview

This lesson contains the following student materials:

Assignment 1 (Parts 1 and 2). Two fictional accounts that raise questions about the extent of freedom U.S. citizens have to speak, march, and protest.

Assignment 2. A brief account of the history and basic goals of the American Nazi party.

Assignment 3. A summary of the requests made by the American Nazi party to stage a march in the predominately Jewish neighborhood of Skokie, Illinois, along with sample arguments for and against allowing the Nazis to stage such a march.

Assignment 4. A summary of the telephone activities of the American Nazi party in Houston, Texas, with sample arguments for and against permitting such recorded telephone messages.

Lesson Objectives

Students will be able to *recognize a problem for inquiry* (To what extent should freedom of speech and the right to parade and protest be exercised in our country?) and *offer hypotheses* in response to this question after discussing Parts 1 and 2 of Assignment 1. *Testing the validity of the hypotheses* will occur as the students examine material in Assignments 2, 3, and 4. Finally, after evaluating the arguments presented in Assignment 4, students will be able to *form and support generalizations* about the extent to which some First and Fourteenth Amendment freedoms should be exercised in our country.

Intended Student Audience: Grades 9-12.

Suggested Time for Classroom Use of Materials: Two to four class periods.

Specific Objectives

Cognitive Objectives. Upon completion of this lesson students will:

knowledge goals
1. Know a brief history of the American Nazi party.
2. Be able to tell why certain activities of the

American Nazi party in 1977-78 raised questions
about the good and bad aspects of the concept of
freedom to speak, march, and demonstrate.

*skill
development*
3. Be able to compare, recall, and interpret information about the application of First and Fourteenth
Amendment freedoms to activities of the American
Nazi party.

4. Recognize this central problem for inquiry: How
far should freedom of speech and the right to
parade and protest extend to our citizens?

5. Be able to form hypotheses in response to the central question for inquiry.

6. Be able to test the validity of the hypotheses by
examining information involving recent activities
(in Skokie, Illinois, and Houston, Texas) of the
American Nazi party.

7. Be able to form and support generalizations about
the extent of freedom of speech and the right to
parade and protest.

Affective Objectives. Upon completion of this lesson students will:

empathy
1. Understand and be able to explain the views of both
those who favor and those who are opposed to allowing extremist organizations to march and demonstrate.

*social
participation*
2. Be willing to participate in group discussions to
examine the question of how much freedom such organizations should have to speak, march, and protest.

*values
clarification*
3. Be willing to attempt to objectively analyze both
their own values and those held by others in regard
to the freedom to speak, protest, and demonstrate.

tolerance
4. Be willing to tolerate (but not necessarily agree
with) a variety of conflicting viewpoints on a controversial topic.

Teaching Suggestions

Introducing the Lesson

This lesson can be introduced in at least two ways. One way would be to ask all the students to consider the two fictional accounts in Assignment 1. As an alternative, you could divide the class into six groups and ask three groups to examine each account.

If the students work in groups, ask each group to read the material presented in the part assigned to it and consider questions 1-5. Each group can then respond to question 6, which calls for students to formulate an abstract question for inquiry. Allow each group to formulate and suggest as many versions as possible. Record these on the chalkboard and ask the entire class to look at the questions formulated by various groups. Are they similar, or are there differences between them? Could any or all of these abstract questions be applied to both situations?

Next, ask volunteers from each group to summarize the situations their groups examined. Then ask the students to consider which of the questions submitted by the various groups would be the most appropriate title for both situations. If it has not already been proposed in some form, suggest this central question for the lesson: How far should freedom of speech and the right to parade or protest extend to our citizens? Ask whether this question adequately summarizes the questions previously submitted. Then have the class supply answers to this central question, along with reasons for their answers.

During the discussion of the lesson's central question, you may wish to have the students read the First and Fourteenth amendments to our federal Constitution. Point out that the First Amendment is a *federal* guarantee of freedom of speech and expression; the Fourteenth Amendment applies such freedoms on a *state* level. Then ask what a "freedom" is. Can freedoms have limits? How far should such freedoms extend? Point out to students that their responses to these questions should be kept in mind as they examine the lesson material about the American Nazi party and some of its recent activities.

Continuing the Lesson

Assignment 2 contains a brief history of the development and basic goals of the American Nazi party. After the assignment has been duplicated, given to the students, and read by them, particular attention should be devoted to the basic goals of the Nazi party. Familiarity with these goals will be essential when students next consider the controversies noted in Assignments 3 and 4.

You may wish to have the class examine Assignment 3 in two parts. First ask the students to read and then discuss with them the introduction to the Skokie, Illinois, situation and other controversies involving the American Nazi party. Once the students understand the background of these situations, they can proceed to the sample arguments for and against the proposed Nazi activities in Skokie. The same format could also be used for the Houston situation (Assignment 4).

When examining the pros and cons of each issue, students should consider the general worth, merit, and reasonableness of each point of view, the arguments that might be made for both sides of the issue, and reasons for their judgments and suggestions.

During the discussion of the pros and cons presented in Assignment 4, ask whether any of them are similar to those included in Assignment 3. Are any different? How might one account for similarities or differences? Are there any similarities between the Skokie and Houston situations and the imaginary stories in Assignment 1? If so, what are they?

For additional information about the Skokie situation, you may wish to point out that the American Nazi party deliberately selected Skokie because half of its 70,000 residents are Jewish and 10 percent are survivors or relatives of survivors of German-Nazi concentration camps during World War II. You might add that when a similar Nazi march occurred in the streets of South St. Louis in March 1978, violence did indeed result. The class could also consider U.S. Supreme Court Justice Oliver Wendell Holmes's 1919 statement that "the most stringent protection of free speech would not protect a man in falsely shouting fire in a theatre and causing a panic."

A summary of the court decisions about the Skokie situation and the role played by the ACLU can be found in March 1978 issue of *Civil Liberties,* the monthly newsletter of the ACLU. The November 1977 issue also contains an explanation of the ACLU's rationale for supporting the Nazis in Skokie--a position that caused the ACLU to incur a drastic loss of membership--in an editorial written by Aryeh Neier, then ACLU executive director, himself a refugee from Nazi Germany. Part of the editorial is reproduced here; you might want to read it to the class and discuss the student's reactions to it.

The ACLU takes all free speech cases. We have always viewed free speech as our prime responsibility. Other cases--prison, mental commitment, juvenile rights, political surveillance, abortion, race and sex discrimination, privacy--require major commitments of resources. Not so with free speech cases. They usually don't require the construction of complete records. They are generally simple and straightforward and it would be untrue to say we don't have the resources to handle them.

ACLU is losing a lot of members and a lot of money because we defend free speech for Nazis. This means . . . that we will have less resources to handle other cases. Is it really so important to defend the rights of Nazis that we are willing to make ourselves less able to defend the rights of others?

The same thought crossed the minds of many of us who make day-to-day decisions for the ACLU. Do a few contemptible Nazis deserve to wreck some important ACLU programs? Some of my colleagues have even wondered out loud whether the real purpose of the Nazis and the KKK is to harm the ACLU by presenting themselves as clients in free-speech cases.

Regardless of such dark speculations, however, we have to recognize what is at stake in Skokie. Skokie tests whether we really believe that free speech must be defended for all--even for those we despise most.

As a Jew, and as a refugee from Nazi Germany, I have strong personal reasons for finding the Nazis repugnant.

Freedom of speech protects my right to denounce Nazis
with all the vehemence I think proper. Free speech also
protected the right of Al Wirin, the ACLU of Southern
California's long-time general counsel, to picket a high
school where a right-wing rally was being held--after
Wirin had won in court a decision allowing the rally to
be held.

If the ACLU does not maintain fidelity to the principle that free speech must be defended for all, we do
not deserve to exist or to call ourselves a civil liberties organization. Caving in to a hostile reaction--
some of it from ACLU members--would only advance the
notion that speakers may be silenced if listeners are
offended. That is the issue in Skokie, as it has been
in a very large number of the free-speech cases the ACLU
has taken on over the years.

Did the Wobblies have a right to speak in company towns?
Did Jehovah's Witnesses or birth-control advocates have
a right to pass out leaflets in Catholic neighborhoods?
Did Norman Thomas have a right to speak in Frank Hague's
Jersey City? Did Paul Robeson have a right to sing at a
concert in Peekskill, New York? Did Martin Luther King,
Jr., have a right to march in Selma, Alabama, or in
Cicero, Illinois?

Did the Jewish Defense League have a right to picket
the Soviet embassy or the home of someone they say was a
Nazi war criminal? Did anti-war demonstrators have a
right to picket the White House? Do Nazis have a right
to hold a demonstration in Skokie?

A lot of the examples I have cited resulted in violence.
Wobblies were murdered in many western cities. Jehovah's
Witnesses were stoned. Norman Thomas narrowly escaped a
lynch mob in Jersey City. There was a riot in Peekskill
and scores of people were injured. Civil-rights marchers

124

were attacked all over the South, in Chicago and its suburbs, and in many other places.

Is any of these instances analogous to shouting fire falsely in a crowded theater? Of course not, although with the advantage of hindsight we know that violence took place. Free speech--as Justice Holmes said and as the great majority of the thousands of letters about Skokie I have received point out--does not protect the shouter of fire. On the contrary, shouting fire falsely in a crowded theater is the antithesis of speech. No other point of view can be heard. A panic takes place too quickly.

By contrast, free speech could operate in Skokie. Opponents of the Nazis are free to speak and to condemn the Nazis. There is no need for opponents of the Nazis to respond violently, but if they do, their violent response is no reason to silence the Nazis. Speakers must not be silenced because their listeners do not like what they say.

It is disheartening to get letters from members quitting the ACLU over defense of free speech for the Nazis and the KKK. These letters ask the ACLU to betray its very reason for existence. I take pride in saying that I detect no weakening of resolve in the ACLU's leadership.

We will continue to defend free speech for everyone. It is costing us a great deal and it is forcing us to cut back on some of the things we should be doing. But if we cannot ourselves hold to the principle that the right to express views must be defended even when the views offend listeners, including ACLU members, we can hardly call on governments to follow that principle. (Reprinted with the permission of Aryeh Neier and the American Civil Liberties Union.)

During a discussion of the Houston situation (Assignment 4), you may want to point out that the Houston chapter of the ACLU decided not to aid the Nazis in their claim to the right to make use of such a recorded telephone message. A majority of the Houston ACLU Board maintained that the First Amendment's constitutional guarantees did not apply to a bounty offer. The class might also need to know that the Nazis did agree to modify the wording of the message, and proposed solutions to these problems.

Optional Teaching Strategies

If you plan to use this lesson early in the school year, you might want to teach it in conjunction with an examination of one or more of the following topics in history:

1. The history of freedom of speech and protest in England.

2. The John Peter Zenger case of 1735.

3. Debates about the passage of the First Amendment to the U.S. Constitution in 1790.

4. Issues raised by the passage of the Alien and Sedition Acts of 1798.

5. Views and decisions about First Amendment freedoms as interpreted by the U.S. Supreme Court since 1919.

6. The history of the U.S. Supreme Court's "clear and present danger" doctrine.

7. The problems and basic constitutional issues posed by the civil-rights demonstrations of the 1960s.

8. Forms of censorship, both legal and informal, as practiced in the United States during World War I, World War II, and the McCarthy era.

Additional Reading

"Again, the Holocaust." *Newsweek,* April 10, 1978, pp. 68-69.

Arkes, Hadley. "Marching Through Skokie." *National Review,* May 12, 1978, pp. 588-593.

Blum, Howard. *Wanted! The Search for Nazis in America.* New York: Fawcett World Library, Crest Books, 1977.

Cowan, Wayne H. "Nazis in America? Process, Due and Overdue." *Christianity and Crisis,* March 7, 1977, pp. 34-36.

"Nazis and the ACLU." *Newsweek,* January 30, 1978, pp. 54-55.

Orlow, Dietrich. *The History of the Nazi Party, 1919-1945,* 2 vols. Pittsburgh: University of Pittsburgh Press, 1969, 1973.

Racist Reader, The, plus accompanying cassette, *The Dangers of Fascism.* Minneapolis: Greenhaven Press, 1974.

"Teaching About the Holocaust." (Seven articles and a selected bibliography.) *Social Education,* April 1978.

STUDENT MATERIALS FOR LESSON 4

WHOSE RIGHTS SHOULD PREVAIL?   TWO DILEMMAS

Part 1

Read about the situation described below and answer the questions that follow.

At Warren High School it is time for student council elections. Two candidates are running for president. Bobby, last year's president, wants to be reelected. He supports the existing school rules and is liked by the teachers and principal.

The other candidate, Mike, is something of a rebel. He would like to do away with the dress code, open up a smoking lounge for students, and get rid of most of the rules governing student behavior. Mike is a good speaker; in fact, some speeches he has made in the past have resulted in demonstrations against the school administration.

Bobby's supporters and some teachers have asked the principal to forbid Mike from making election campaign speeches. A school bond issue is coming up, and they are anxious to avoid the unfavorable publicity that a demonstration would create. The principal agrees.

Mike and his supporters refuse to accept this ruling. Mike says that his rights to campaign should not be restricted simply because of the actions that happen after his speeches. He points out that as an American citizen, his right to free speech is guaranteed by the Bill of Rights in the U.S. Constitution.

The issue goes to the school board for resolution. Imagine that you are the president of the school board, and answer the following questions:

Questions

1. What does Mike want to do if he is elected president of the student council?

2.   Why does Mike think that he should be allowed to speak?

3.   Who is Mike's opponent in the student council election?

4.   What did Bobby's supporters want the principal to do? Why?

5.   How would you resolve this dispute? Why?

6.   What sort of question do you think this situation might raise?
(In framing your question, do <u>not</u> use the words "Bobby," "Mike," "student
council election," or "principal.")

Part 2

Read about the situation described below and answer the questions
that follow.

Daviston, Georgia, is a community of approximately 100,000 people.
Most of them are descended from veterans of the Confederate army.

In nearby Atlanta, a few hundred former northerners belong to the
Association of Northern Patriots, an organization consisting of the
descendants of Gen. William T. Sherman's Union army. General Sherman and
his Union troops did great damage to Georgia during the Civil War.

The Association of Northern Patriots wants to have a parade to com-
memorate the surrender of the Confederate army on April 9, 1965, at
Appomattox. Besides displaying floats depicting the surrender of the
South and anti-Confederacy slogans and posters, they are planning to play
"Marching Through Georgia" all along the parade route, which will begin
in Atlanta and go through Daviston.

The Ku Klux Klan and the residents of Daviston have obtained a
court injunction to prevent the parade from taking place. Those who
oppose the parade have threatened to hold a violent demonstration
if the injunction is not obeyed.

The Association of Northern Patriots has appealed the case to the
state supreme court, saying that the First Amendment to the U.S. Const-
tution guarantees their right to parade even at the risk of inciting a
riot. Imagine that you are a state supreme court justice, and consider
how you would resolve this dispute.

Questions

1. What is the Association of Northern Patriots? What do its
members want to do?

2. Who opposes what the ANP wants to do? Why?

3. Do you think that people should be allowed to say or sing anything they please while marching on a public street? Why?

4. Do you think that violent demonstrations are justified if the issue is important enough?

5. If you were a member of the state supreme court, how would you vote on this issue? Why?

6. What sort of questions do you think this lesson might raise? (In framing your question, do *not* use the terms "Confederate," "patriotic organization," "ANP," "Sherman," "Ku Klux Klan," or "Georgia.")

A BRIEF HISTORY OF THE AMERICAN NAZIS

Read the brief history of the American Nazi party below and answer the questions that follow.

The American Nazi party in America was an outgrowth of the National Socialist movement in Germany during the late 1920s and early 1930s.

Adolph Hitler, the leader of the German Nazi party until his death in 1945, became a dominant figure in Germany in the late 1920s as a result of his recovery philosophy for the World War I-crushed nation. He played on people's fears and hatred of foreigners--of anyone who was not what he regarded as a "true-blooded German." His racial philosophy was a major tenet of the National Socialist German Workers Party (abbreviated "NAZI").

In the United States, the Nazi movement began with the formation of the German-American Bund (union), a group whose members wore German military uniforms and asserted their cultural oneness with their country of origin. Gradually, the Bund aligned itself fully with Nazi military philosophies. During World War II, many Bundists fought for Germany against America.

After the war the Bund retained its separate existence under the leadership of George Lincoln Rockwell and eventually changed its name to the American Nazi party. Today's American Nazi party is a white supremist group similar to the Ku Klux Klan.

While most of its members do not advocate concentration camps or wholesale slaughter for non-Germans, as Hitler did, only whites of Western European heritage are admitted to membership. Although the American Nazi party is a small group, because of its policies and activities it is often in the news.

Questions

1. What is the American Nazi party? Where and why did it start? What relation did it have to the Nazi party of Germany?

2. What are the major policies of the American Nazi party?

3. What do you think of the American Nazi party? Why?

Lesson 4, Assignment 3

THE SKOKIE CASE: BACKGROUND AND ARGUMENTS

This assignment contains some background information about the Skokie case and sample arguments both for and against the American Nazi party's position. Read all the material and then answer the questions at the end of the assignment.

In 1977 the American Nazi party applied to the city council of Skokie, Illinois, for a permit to hold a march through the city. This request met with strong opposition, particularly from the Jewish residents of Skokie.

The Nazi party was told that the permit would be granted only if the party would agree to post a large bond to ensure that the march would not result in violence. Since it was not standard procedure to demand that such a bond be posted, the Nazis felt that they were being discriminated against because of their political beliefs, and they appealed to the courts.

In early 1978 both the Illinois State Supreme Court and a federal district court judge in Chicago ruled that the Nazis should not have to post bond, given the fact that other groups did not have to meet such a requirement. The Nazis decided to continue with their plans to march in Skokie. Skokie city officials appealed to the U.S. Supreme Court.

On June 12, 1978, by a 7-2 vote, the U.S. Supreme Court ruled that Skokie officials could not turn down the Nazis' request to march. Just after that ruling the American Nazi leader, Frank Collins, canceled plans for the Skokie march and announced that one would be held in Chicago. American Nazis subsequently held two separate rallies in Chicago--one on June 24 at the plaza in front of the main federal building and one on July at Marquette Park--with the approval of the U.S. Supreme Court. At both of the Chicago rallies, hundreds of demonstrators chanted anti-Nazi slogans during Collins' speeches, but there was no violence other than some minor scuffling.

The Nazis' request to march in Skokie raised some basic questions about the extent to which the freedoms guaranteed in the First and Fourteenth amendments pertain to all U.S. citizens. Here are some sample arguments for and against allowing the Nazis to march in Skokie. As you examine them, think about which ones seem the *most* reasonable and which seem the *least* reasonable.

Arguments for the Nazis' right to march	Arguments against the Nazis' right to march
The First and Fourteenth amendments to our U.S. Constitution guarantee freedom of speech, expression, and association; this freedom includes the right to march.	The courts have ruled that these freedoms are not absolute when a proposed activity is shown to be "likely to produce a clear and present danger of a serious substantive evil that rises far above public inconvenience, annoyance, or unrest."
In order to protect everyone's rights, we must protect the rights of those whom we agree with least-- no exceptions.	Each situation should be considered separately. Each case should be decided on its own merits.
No matter what a person's opinion, it's his or her undeniable right to express it.	The American Nazis are calling for an end to "justice for all" with their white-supremacy policies and their discriminatory views about nonwhites and Jews.
There are many historical precedents for letting dissident groups stage protest marches in spite of the opposition of other citizens. Many southerners opposed the civil-rights marches of the 1960s.	The Nazis are an anti-Semitic group. In World War II, Nazi Germany was responsible for killing 6 million Jews. The population of Skokie is heavily Jewish, and many residents lost friends and relatives in Nazi concentration camps.

The Nazis promise that their march will be peaceful.

The Jewish people of Skokie say that the march would remind them of World War II and stir up strong feelings that might lead to violent action.

Questions

1. Of the arguments presented above, which individual ones do you think are the most valid or most reasonable? Which do you feel are the least valid or reasonable? Why?

2. Which side has the best case? Why?

3. In your opinion, should the Nazis be allowed to march in Skokie? If so, should they abide by any special rules? Explain your reasons.

THE HOUSTON CASE: BACKGROUND AND ARGUMENTS

This assignment presents some background information about the
Houston case, along with some sample arguments for and against the Nazis'
position. Read the material and answer the questions that follow.

In November 1977 the American Nazi party offered for public con-
sumption a tape-recorded telephone message to residents of the Houston
area. The recorded message offered a $5,000 bounty for each nonwhite
killed in the act of attacking a white person while breaking into a white-
owned home or business. After numerous complaints and a civil suit, a
district court judge issued a restraining order to keep the recording
from being played in its current form. The judge specifically ordered
that all references in the recording to killings or rewards for killings
be deleted. The text of the tape-recorded message was as follows:

> This is the voice of the White Race Security Officer
> speaking. We are calling for an all-out war against Jews
> and other nonwhites that seek the destruction of our race.
> I am sure you all realize that the illegal nonwhite immi-
> grants have overrun our borders and colored hordes have
> made us flee to the suburbs of our cities. We are begin-
> ning the battle by offering a $5,000 prize for every non-
> white killed during an attack on a white person. . . .
> We are tired of babysitting the weak and ignorant of
> our race. . . . If you believe yourself capable to join
> the fight and put on the brown shirt and swastika as a
> symbol of your dedication, then join with us. Dial 476-
> 5156, and I will make sure your efforts will be rewarded
> and your future will look brighter not only for your own
> personal satisfaction but for the future of all civili-
> zation.
> We will note and long remember the death of our racial
> comrades both at home and abroad. They have given their

lives to free us from international Jewry, and it is
our obligation to carry forth the battle to every
part of this globe. Jew and coloreds' blood will
mix in the streets as white men and women get their
scores settled for all the years of hell the hordes
have given them. Jews will be the ones to suffer
the most for their part in importing the colored
hordes for cheap labor without regard for the devas-
tation it has ultimately caused. Dial 476-5156 to
claim your reward for the carcass of any nonwhite
killed in an attack. If you decide to join the
fight, I will be waiting for your call, so please
make your decision now. The time of our cause is at
hand, and the American white race will stand and be
counted for their God and country and for their
glorious heritage--white power and white victory.

Now that you have read what the tape-recorded message contained,
consider some sample arguments for and against letting it be used.

Arguments for its use

Under the First and Fourteenth
amendments to the U.S. Constitution,
the Nazis have the right to free
speech. On this point, one American Nazi stated: "If we have
reached the low of being told what
words to say, what ideas to use,
then we have been left no alternatives but to take off the
restraints of our freedoms with
force, if necessary."

Arguments against its use

No one has a constitutional
right to say whatever he or she
pleases at any time in any
place. It is against the law,
for example, to shout "Fire!"
in a crowded theater when there
is no fire, nor may anyone
deliberately incite a riot or
other unlawful disturbance.
The Nazis have no right to wave
their hatred in the faces of
American Jews and blacks, any
more than people have the right
to expose themselves in a public

The Nazis have not actively contracted to have anyone killed. They are not even calling people on the phone. In order to learn of the offer, it is necessary to call their number.

The offer may be considered to be a businessperson's protection measure. Money is being offered to help cut down on the amount of crime.

area--both actions are forms of self-expression.

Whatever the method, money is being offered for the killing of people. Such an offer is of questionable legality. Moreover, because of the extremely emotional nature of the issue, the message could easily incite people to violence.

The offer applies only to certain racial and ethnic groups, whereas criminal acts are committed by people from every group. Besides, laws should be enforced by authorized officials and agencies, not by vigilante committees.

Questions

1. What, exactly, did the tape-recorded message by the Nazis really say? How many points can you list about it?

2. Do you think that any of the "facts" cited in the message are incorrect or distorted? How might you begin to determine that?

3. What is "propaganda"? Do you think there is any propaganda in the Nazi message? How might you determine whether there is?

4. Which of the sample arguments provided do you feel have the greatest merit or validity? Why? Which ones do you feel have the least merit or validity? Why?

5. What other arguments could be added to these sample pros and cons? Could any of the arguments used in the Skokie case (Assignment 3) be applied to the Houston situation? Explain your answer.

6. Suppose you were the judge who was asked to rule on the use of the Nazi telephone message. What would you have decided, and why?

7. At this point, how far do you think freedom of speech and the right to parade and protest should extend to all citizens? Give reasons for your answer.